Debbie's Stories

Debbie's Stories

Moe Liss

YBK Publishers
New York

Debbie's Stories

Copyright © 2003
by Moe Liss

All rights reserved
including the right of reproduction
in whole or in part in any form

YBK Publishers
425 Broome St.
New York, NY 10013

ISBN 0-9703923-5-4

Library of Congress Control Number: 2003109085

Manufactured in the United States of America

ver 3-07

Contents

Preface	vii
Dedication	ix
Introduction	xi
Debbie's First Love	1
Debbie's Eighth Birthday	3
The Opera	6
How Eileen Came Into Our Lives	10
Eileen's Stories	12
First Legal Drink	16
Cheaper To Grow It Than To Buy It	18
David's Stories	21
Ethel's (David's Mother) Stories	23
Debbie Gives Daddy Permission	25
Coping With An Incurable Disease	28
Las Vegas	30
Toni's Stories	32
Opening Day At Shea	34
It Will Hurt You More Than It Will Hurt Me	36
Baseball	38
Lupus Convention 1987, Chicago, Illinois	42
Fighting For The Rights Of Lupus Patients	44
Debbie, Pearl and My Mom	48
Debbie's 30th Birthday	51
Debbie and Desert Storm	55
The Birth of Debbie's Niece, Ronit	58
Introduction to Debbie and Gershon	60
Pearl's Stories	62
Josie's (Pearl's Mom) Story	69

Another "Bubba" Story	70
Jeff Liss' Stories	73
The Meaning of My Life	75
Debbie's Gifts (Aunt Rose and Uncle Murray)	88
The Dream	89
Today Is The First Day Of The Rest Of Your Life	91
Debbie's Team	93
The Mets Flag.	97
Letters to Dad From Jeff	100
Letter to Moe From Shannon	101
Afterthoughts	103
Afterwards	104

Preface

My daughter Debra Liss passed away on August 19, 1996, ten days beyond her thirty-seventh birthday, in Haifa, Israel. I was there at her side, on that most painful day of my life. Although the final cause of her death was lung cancer—she had been diagnosed four months earlier with that dreaded disease—Debbie had suffered first with lupus and then scleroderma for 16 years.

These years since her passing have been a struggle for me; there have been times when I really didn't want to go on living—times when the pain was so great, I felt there had to be another way. If it weren't for my wife Pearl, my three other children, Brenda, Jeff and Jaime, granddaughters Ronit and Shai, sister Rose and brother-in-law Murray and my other close friends and relatives, I don't know how I could have gotten to this point to write *Debbie's Stories*.

This book probably would never have come to be if it weren't for a phone call I received from Doris, a member of one of the lupus rap groups that my wife Pearl and I facilitate. It was a Saturday morning—I remember that morning very well—when the phone rang. Doris said "Good morning, Moe, I really enjoyed the story that you told about Debbie at our last meeting. [I have been telling Debbie's Stories to anyone who would listen since she passed away]. I hope this doesn't offend you, but have you ever thought about writing a book of Debbie's stories? You know how much I love to hear you tell the stories, and I know everyone in the group feels the same way. I think there might be many people out there who would enjoy reading Debbie's stories." Wow—I said. I never thought about that—and that really is food for thought—thank you so much for calling! She hung up, I hung up and I turned to Pearl and said, "you won't believe this." I retold the phone conversation with Doris. Pearl thought it would be a great project; it might even be good therapy for me, and it might also help other people. She wasn't sure I *could* work on such a project; would it be too painful? It would bring back both painful and beautiful memories, and could I really follow through? At that moment I didn't know. It was just a thought and for a while I didn't seriously pursue it.

It was about one month after the phone call that I mentioned it at the lupus group, with thanks to Doris of course; and received a tremendous amount of support from the folks attending. I then began thinking seriously about writing this book.

So: I first want to thank Doris for the idea. I especially want to thank my loving, beautiful, supportive, caring wife, Pearl for everything she has given me, not only over these seven years since Debbie's passing, but also all the years that we have been together. Thanks to my children, grandchildren, family and friends for their support, and especially to the people of The Compassionate Friends, to whom this book is dedicated.

Dedication

I dedicate this book to The Compassionate Friends, an international organization of parents who have lost children. Specifically, the Wyckoff, New Jersey Chapter of The Compassionate Friends, and all the beautiful and wonderful people I have met over these years at our Tuesday meetings.

In November 1996, Pearl, who had been doing research on groups and organizations that might help me to cope with this great loss and might ease some of the pain that we were both suffering, came upon a group called The Compassionate Friends. She thought it might fit the bill as a group we both could relate to. We had no idea what the meetings were about or what to expect.

I will never forget my first meeting—the fourth Tuesday in November 1996.

We walked into a very large hall at the Christian Health Care Center in Wyckoff, New Jersey. Ann Marie greeted us warmly. She took our personal information and made every effort to comfort us. What struck me first was that in this very large room there were circles of chairs, maybe seven or eight circles, each consisting of eight to ten chairs. We got there early—about 7:10 PM. The meeting doesn't officially start till about 7:30 to 7:45 PM. As we filled out the information cards and talked with Ann Marie, we were amazed by the number of people who began entering that hall and filling up each of the circles. *My God, I can't believe that these are all parents who lost children!* There must have been 70 or 80 that first evening. Pearl and I sat down at one of the circles, where Ann Marie was the facilitator. She introduced herself and said a few words about who The Compassionate Friends were and indicated that each one of us, if we chose to, could share a little bit about who we were and why we came, and that there was no pressure to talk, if we did not want to. When it came to us, Pearl deferred to me and I said, "My name is Moe; this is my wife Pearl; our daughter Debbie passed away from lung cancer three months ago and that is why we are here."

As those in the group proceeded to introduce themselves and tell why they were there, it was difficult to absorb the stories that we heard. Each story about the death of a child, regardless of their age or the circumstances that caused their death, brought even more pain to both Pearl and me.

That was the first of many Compassionate Friends meetings both Pearl and I have participated in. We have become close to a number of people and they to us. I am saying this from the heart, that if it wasn't for those meetings, especially the people, and the love and support from my wife Pearl, I don't know how I could have made it. I therefore dedicate this book to all The Compassionate Friends in the Wyckoff, New Jersey Support Group and all The Compassionate Friends throughout the world. We share each other's pain and this book is dedicated to each one of you. If reading *Debbie's Stories* gives you a moment of laughter, a moment where you shed a tear, a moment where you may compare some of the stories to stories of your children; if it touches you in any way, if it helps you get through another day; then writing *Debbie's Stories* will have fulfilled my promise. The promise of keeping her always alive inside of me and through her, touching each and every one of you. I love telling "Debbie Stories," and I hope you will be enriched by reading them.

Introduction

This book is not a biography of my daughter Debbie, although the stories are biographical in nature, in that they describe many of the moments of her beautiful life. Some of them are very humorous; a few might be a little embarrassing—but I have her permission. I speak to her just about every day. If some happen to touch a note of embarrassment to some of her friends, I also have permission from these friends to tell these stories. Some are serious and some sad, maybe a tear or two will be shed; that is all part of her life.

The stories are told in the first person. I, her father, will tell many of them. There are stories told by my wife Pearl, Debbie's brother Jeff, her Aunt Rose and Uncle Murray, and by Debbie's close friends Eileen, Toni, Ethel and David. In the chapter heading of each story, credit is given to the person telling the story. If no one's name is shown, then I am the teller. *Debbie's Stories* is a joint composition by the people who loved her and whom she loved, the people that touched her life and that she touched in return, the impact she made on our lives—just a little bit about Debbie, our beautiful Debbie.

Debbie's First Love

This story begins in the early sixties, when Debbie's Grandpa and Bubba purchased a bungalow in the small town of Livingston Manor, New York, in the Catskill Mountains. They bought it so their children and grandchildren would have a place to go on weekends, vacations and holidays. It was a really cute, small cottage with a kitchenette and a couple of bedrooms. A little swimming pool, more like a swimming hole, a "social hall" with a ping-pong table and a horse-shoe pitch, and about twelve other units made up this bungalow colony. It was called Ram's Bungalows, after the owner's name. My sister and brother-in-law and their twin sons, Barry and Michael, as well as my family, would use the bungalow throughout the summer months. Of course, when Debbie's Grandpa and Bubba were there, it was even more special because then we would all receive very special treatment, including the best home-cooked meals in the country. One of the highlights of going to the bungalow was blueberry picking with Grandpa; he loved to pick blueberries and those blueberries would eventually become blueberry pie, cake, or muffins, since Bubba was a wonderful baker as well as a cook. Bubba created great pastries out of those blueberries.

Down the road from the Bungalow Colony was a small farm, called Lena's Farm, which had dairy cows, chickens and other animals. Every now and then we would walk down the hill to show our children the animals. The children loved animals, we enjoyed the hike and they were nice neighbors. One day in 1966, I believe while the rest of us were picking blueberries Debbie walked down to the farm. At this point, Debbie was not really a blueberry picker, she was more inclined "to do her own thing," while Brenda, Jeff, Grandpa, Bubba and I were doing our blueberry picking. On her way to Lena's Farm, Debbie meets a little boy named Freddie, who was about her age or a year older. These two youngsters, Debbie and Freddie, really hit it off. I don't know what they talked about, but I know that when Debbie came back that afternoon, all she talked about was meeting this young boy and how she wanted to play with him. For most of that summer, whenever we went to the Bungalow, Debbie would spend time with Freddie. In fact, she even mentioned the "L" word, and this was the first time we heard the word from her—"you know I really love him." Toward the end of the summer the two planned a big date. They wanted to go to the movies; there was a movie theatre in the town of Roscoe, very near Livingston Manor. (There is also a famous diner, called Roscoe's Diner—which is still famous today.) Their plans included going to the movies and then going out for ice cream. That was Debbie's first date. I remember taking the two to the movies and after the movies going to Roscoe's Diner, where they had ice cream. The two of them couldn't keep their eyes off one another. We can consider it a first date . . . first love ? Well, we can say for sure that at age 7, Debbie began to notice that there was such a thing as the opposite sex. I know throughout her life Debbie was interested in romance, she was a true romantic. I sincerely believe that one of the major disappointments in Debbie's life was that, even though she had many relationships, she never married or had a family. I am certain that was very painful to her.

Debbie's Eighth Birthday

Birthdays were really important for all of our children. Celebrating them as a milestone in their life, sharing with friends and family, were very, very important. When Debbie turned 8 she wanted to have a special birthday party. As an avid baseball fan and even more, an avid Met fan, Debbie wanted to have her birthday celebrated at Shea Stadium. The order was given for her Daddy to make arrangements to have dinner at the Diamond Club, which was a very exclusive restaurant. To dine there, you need some kind of membership, be a season ticket holder or guest of some sport celebrity to obtain entrance. The other order was that she would like to take a picture with her favorite Met, who at that time was Ron Swoboda. That was a tall order, but for Debbie, Daddy could always create miracles and that was what Daddies were there for. That was the order I received the summer of 1967, for her eighth birthday, on August 9.

During that period of my life, I was coordinating Federal Programs in Education for the Paterson Board of Education. The summer of 1967 would go down as one of the most violent summers in our nation's history. A summer of civil rights demonstrations, counter demonstrations and actual street battles in many of our major urban centers. I had designed and developed, for the City of Paterson, a summer program to involve over 3000 students and 200 to 300 teachers who were hired to work with our youngsters, not only to involve them in productive activities of a social, educational and recreational nature, but to make certain that the streets of Paterson were kept cool. One of the members of my staff that summer was a fellow by the name of Frank Bannister. Frank told me he was an ex-ballplayer who worked in the Mets minor league system and eventually became a bull pen catcher for the Mets. He mentioned he had these great connections with the Mets and if I ever needed Mets tickets, he would take care of me. I went to Frank and told him of my daughter Debbie's desire for her eighth Birthday. She wanted to have dinner in the Diamond Club, have a picture taken with her favorite, Ron Swoboda and, of course, then to have special box seats to view the game. Frank said,

"That's fine, I'll take care of it." I was a little skeptical. "You will," I said, and he said, "Yeah. August ninth, it's a home game. I will have everything arranged in your name and you will be my guests. Just take all your kids and go to the entrance to the Diamond Club. Your name will be on the list, you will go up to the Diamond Club and then after dinner you will go on the field to have pictures taken not only with Debbie and her favorite player but, what about your other children?" I said that Brenda liked Cleon Jones and Jeff liked Ed Kranepool. He said, "I will make sure that those players are out on the field and I will have a photographer waiting to take their picture." To tell you the truth, I didn't fully believe that Frank Banister could arrange all these things. But he swore to me that he would do that. Just get your kids and family to Shea Stadium on the ninth of August and this will be arranged. I thought, well, this is worth a shot. I went home and told Debbie, your wish has been fulfilled.

August 9, 1967, arrived, and we headed for Shea Stadium. We were pretty dressed up for Debbie's Birthday, dinner at the Diamond Club and pictures on the field of Shea Stadium. Sure enough, when I got to the gate, our name was on the list. We proceeded up to the Diamond Club, a very beautiful restaurant overlooking the field. We sat down to a wonderful dinner and a birthday cake with candles that had been ordered in Debbie's honor. We sang Happy Birthday and she was thrilled. Then I said to the waiter, "I understand that we have an arrangement to go on the field and take pictures." Sure enough, there was an escort for us to go down the elevator to the entrance to the field. This was unbelievable for the kids since they had never been on the field of a major league ballpark. Within a moment or two, three Met players came out of the dugout—Ron Swoboda, Cleon Jones and Ed Kranepool, exactly as requested. The players introduced themselves to me and to my children and signed their autograph books. Then, lo and behold, an official Met photographer came out and said, O.K. now I'm ready to take the photo. On the following page you will see the photograph taken of Brenda, Debbie and Jeff, each with their favorite ballplayer. Who says miracles never happen? One happened that day.

I will always be indebted to Frank Bannister for making Debbie's Eighth Birthday such a memorable occasion. I know my children never forgot that day. The photo that you are viewing now was taken from Debbie's home after she passed away; it is now in my home and forever will be a beautiful memory of that wonderful, wonderful day.

Debbie, Jeff, and Brenda with Mets ballplayers

The Opera

I had purchased a subscription to the Metropolitan Opera in the early 1960's with the intention of exposing my children to some of the finer things in life. As it turned out, Debbie and her older sister Brenda loved going to the opera. Jeff didn't become that interested in music; sports were his thing.

Debbie and Brenda both played the piano; Brenda, later on played the clarinet in both her high school and college bands. Debbie, besides playing the piano, also took up the guitar; she loved playing the guitar. This particular story about Debbie and the opera happened when Debbie was eight years old.

I don't know whether Debbie enjoyed the opera for itself or whether it was the dressing up and going out with her Daddy to New York City, having lunch and then going to the opera. Regardless of her motivation, she did accompany me on a number of occasions and this story is about one of her first operas, Mozart's "The Marriage of Figaro."

Whenever I took either Debbie or Brenda to the opera, I'd make sure to go over the story in advance. Operas are sung, of course, in the language of the composer or the language of that particular material and this was before "supertitles" in English. The "Marriage of Figaro" was sung in Italian. Since Mozart operas always involve plots and sub-plots, it was important that they came prepared with some basic understanding of the opera.

Debbie enjoyed the music, and she enjoyed the story, especially the romantic comedy aspects; at age eight, Debbie was really into romance and boy-girl relationships. At that time Debbie was in the third grade at School Number 26 in Paterson, New Jersey. Her class had an activity called "show and tell" where the teacher would ask the children to bring something in and tell about it. Debbie chose to bring in the program from the opera and tell the story. My work at that time gave me the flexibility of time. When I found out she was going to do her "show and tell" on the opera, I managed to be there to see how my eight-year-old daughter would tell the very convoluted plot of this opera.

Debbie got up in front of the class, showed the program of the opera and then continues on to the following… "On Saturday, my father took me to see this opera and I am going to tell you the main story. See, this was a story about this Count who really didn't like his wife and he really liked Susanna. Now Susanna was going to get married to Figaro and Figaro found out that the Count had eyes for his wife-to-be, Susanna. Now the Countess also was very jealous of the fact that her husband was not giving her much attention so anyway Figaro, the Countess and Susanna decided that they would trick the Count. What they would do is, they wanted to show that the Count was really, really a bad man because he was flirting with Susanna and they wanted to catch him. So what happens was the Countess got dressed up as Susanna and she went into the garden and the Count thought he was really proposing his love to Susanna but he was really doing it to his wife. See, the Countess was dressed up as Susanna, behind the bushes was the real Susanna and Figaro laughing and laughing because they are going to catch the Count cheating on his wife. So sure enough the Count came out and started singing this beautiful love song to Susanna who was really his wife, dressed up as Susanna. Then finally after he finished she takes off her disguise and shows that she is rally his wife and not Susanna everybody came out and the Count was really embarrassed and he asked his wife to forgive him and that he really loves her and that he will never put eyes on Susanna again and guess what, they all sang and everyone made up."

Sitting in the back of the room listening to my eight-year-old tell this story, I see all the other children are laughing and smirking and the teacher is turning colors as Debbie describes how this guy is trying to get another man's wife. Debbie just went on and on like it was neighborhood gossip, and finally the teacher said, "Debbie that was great; but I hope your father takes you to another kind of opera next time."

Here's another opera story.

When she was 12 years old in seventh grade, Debbie was taking German as her foreign language. She came up to me and said "Daddy, I would like to see a German opera so that I can practice my German. Is there an opera this season on your subscription that is German?" Well, yes, there was a German opera on my subscription that year, it was Wagner's "Tristan and Isolde." Those who know opera, you know that it is a very long opera, lasting about five hours. I really had no desire to take Debbie to see this opera, since I didn't believe she would either understand it or be able to sit through five hours of Wagner. But she pleaded with me, "Please, Daddy give me the tickets because my girlfriend and I both want to see a German opera and see how much we can understand." If you knew Debbie, you grasped that when she pleaded and begged you had to give in, and so, very reluctantly, I said, "I tell you what I'll do—I will take you and your girlfriend into New York. It's was an early opera, starting at 12:30 in the afternoon, so we will have an early lunch and then you can go and see the opera. I know the times that each of the acts will end, so if you happen to feel you can't take it anymore, you're bored or whatever, you come out and I will be waiting for you." I really didn't think she would stay for the whole opera.

It was a very cold and sunny day, the three of us went into the City and had lunch. Both girls were very dressed up. I gave them the tickets, bid them goodbye and they went into the opera house. I'm out there saying to myself they won't last beyond one act. At that time, and still today, once you go into the opera house you are not to leave during an act, you must wait until the end of the act. I continued to be sure they wouldn't make it past the first act, so at the time the first act was to end I went to the front of the Met and waited for them to come out. I waited for a good while as our seats were in the balcony, four tiers up, but the girls never appeared. I couldn't believe it. Where were they? Were they that enthralled with the opera? I did some more walking around Manhattan and thought, "I know that they would definitely be out after the second act." I came back again and waited in the front of the Met, and waited and waited and again, no Debbie and friend. I knew she wasn't understanding a word of it because even if she had a great command of the German language, which she didn't, it would be difficult to understand as sung—even if it was in English you'd not understand it. So now I'm *really* wondering why she's not there. I was certain the music wasn't going to thrill her and it is a very long and involved opera.

I thought, well this must be some kind of miracle.

I left, did some shopping and came back at the end of the opera. It was now dark out, wintertime, about 5:30 PM. The opera is letting out and I can't wait to hear the stories of how she enjoyed this great opera because she stayed there five-plus hours. I see her coming down the stairs, with her girlfriend. I see her face and it was not a happy face, her face looked very angry.

I say, "Well, how did you guys enjoy the opera?"

"Daddy," she said angrily, "where were you?"

"What do you mean, where was I?"

"We came out after the first act. We were ready to go home and we waited for you."

"I was waiting for you downstairs," I said.

Downstairs," she cried out, "we were waiting for you upstairs. We thought you would come upstairs and bring us down."

I said, "Are you telling me that you came out and waited and waited upstairs? Why didn't you come downstairs? I waited for you outside the Opera House after each act."

The story was that she was expecting me to go upstairs and escort her down while I instead was outside the Met, waiting for her to come down. She came out after each act, getting angrier and angrier. Where was I, I promised her I would be there waiting. She was afraid that if she went downstairs she would have to go outside and wouldn't be able to get back in. It was cold out, so rather than be out in the cold they would sit through this boring, long opera—at least they'd be warm.

Debbie said, "I will *never* go to another opera again! Why did you torture me?" I meekly said, "I'm sorry for the mix up; I'll make up for it. Let's go out and have dinner."

How Eileen Came Into Our Lives

Debbie and Eileen were probably the oldest and closest of friends from the time Debbie was 15 to the time she passed away—more than 20 years of friendship. I wish to tell you a little bit about that relationship and especially my involvement with that relationship.

Eileen was one of 3 daughters of parents who were divorced. She lived with her mother in East Brunswick, N.J., a few blocks away from where Debbie lived. This was 1974, at that time I worked for an organization called COPE, Inc. doing some exciting work in behavioral changes with schools systems, prisons and industry. I remember coming home from work—I was working with the Philadelphia Prison System—that Friday afternoon about 5:30. I walked into our home and there were Debbie and Eileen sitting in the living room.

I knew Eileen well; she was Debbie's closest friend and she had been at our home many times. I walked in, gave them both a hug and Debbie then said, "I have something very important to tell you." She proceeded to say that Eileen would like to spend the weekend here. She had been over before, nothing wrong with that—I said fine. I said, "does her mother know?"

Debbie said, "No she does not."

I then said, "Just call and tell her mother that she would be staying."

Debbie said, "Daddy, she really doesn't want to go home."

Well now, we are not talking about a weekend.

"What do you mean she doesn't want to go home?"

"Daddy, she wants to live with us for awhile."

Wow! I mean, can you imagine? I said, "Hold on what is going on here."

Debbie said, "You know the home situation isn't good for Eileen and she is not doing well in school, and she thinks that this would be a better place for her to stay." She goes on and on and, "Daddy, please don't send her home." Debbie is now pleading the case for Eileen—who is a very lovely girl. "I spoke with Eileen and she said she would like to live with us and would you call her mother and tell her."

Well, I get on the phone and I call her mom and explain the situation. I let her mom know that her daughter is O.K. and that she would like to spend the weekend; I didn't want to commit to anything more. Her mother says, that's fine, whatever she wants, she wasn't going to argue with Eileen.

That weekend lasted about 5 or 6 months; in fact, Eileen became my foster child. I like to feel that in those months Eileen spent with us we developed a special relationship, a relationship that we still have today (Eileen is married now with a family of her own.) I know it was special for the girls; they lived in the same room and got even closer as they bonded. That special bond is still there today, even though Debbie is no longer with us.

Eileen's Stories

The first thing I have to say is that I do have Debbie stories to tell. The one thing I would say overall about my relationship with Debbie is that over the years we did things together. When we were in East Brunswick High School and then afterwards, we had what I would call a cerebral and a soul relationship. It was the kind of relationship where if we didn't talk for three, four months—I think the longest we ever went was six months without talking to one another—it never seemed to matter. Maybe for the first ten seconds of a new conversation there would be that pause after "How are you?" Then it would tumble the way it always had. So my stories would be a little bit different from those of her friends in California, the people she actually hung around with. When Debbie and I were adults we were not hanging out together. I did make two trips to California, and one of my Debbie Stories is about how, for one of my trips, I called her spur of the moment and said, "You know what, I really need to get away and I was going to come visit you. I want to see if I can get a flight—is that O.K.?" Debbie said yes. I went over Easter break. During that trip she dug her guitar out of its case, and some old music. I want to tell you one thing I always remembered was the song Debbie learned, I know it was from her Youth Group days, *Let Me Be A Little Kinder*. You know, I still remember that song. I don't remember all the words but I remember, "Let me be a little kinder, Let me be a little blinder to the faults I see around me, Let me be a little more." Isn't it wild that I still remember that?

Somehow, when we were fifteen years old, we got it into our heads that we could write a song. Debbie played the guitar and I loved to write, so we thought she could write the music and I could write the words. I can't remember how long we spent on it. I just know it was a LONG time. We practiced, we rewrote, we "polished" it. Finally, we were ready for our debut. It was a very long song, although we didn't realize, at 15, just how long it was.

We invited Debbie's dad downstairs to our room to listen to it. Debbie played and we both sang. Well, this thing had sooooo many choruses.

Beginning after about the third one, Debbie's dad would say, "That was really great" and he'd clap and Debbie would be strumming and Debbie would say "no, no" and she would do another verse. Then there was a bridge and Debbie's dad would say, "you were really great," (but I think he couldn't wait to go upstairs—no such luck..) Next verse it actually looked like a scene from a Saturday Night Live Sketch. Debbie is like, no, there's more and we just kept singing and singing and singing. He would think it was over and we kept singing and singing and singing (picture the Energizer bunny.) Finally it was over and we couldn't understand why he didn't ask for an encore. Fast forward a decade I was in California visiting Debbie. One night we were feeling a little good and Debbie decided to take out the old guitar. Rummaging through her music, sure enough, there was our song, our masterpiece. Hey, maybe Arista might be interested, you never know. So we decided to perform it. At one point, after one of the many verses, one of us said, "Oh my God, doesn't this thing ever end???" And it was absolutely AWFUL! I mean, we didn't know if we should laugh or cry. Of course, we did a little bit of both. It's such a little memory, a moment, but the kind that stays with you. We teased each other about the song many times after that. We certainly knew never to quit our day jobs!!

    I think the whole point is that it's moments that make up a lifetime. No matter how brief the moment, no matter how brief the lifetime. They stack up against each other like cards in a deck. We can shuffle the cards and pull them out, one at a time to look at, to analyze, but best of all, to relive. Not that this ever makes up for the loss. Solitaire can be a very lonely game, and memories are a poor substitute for the real thing. But thank God for those memories. Anyway, Thank God for those moments. For however brief they are, they are ours, and no one can take them away. NO ONE NOT EVER.

    I remember the first time I met Debbie..it was a fairly warm evening. We were on Ryders Lane in East Brunswick, New Jersey. "You've probably never hitch-hiked before," her words rang out. Who is this little pipsqueak of a person anyway, I thought.

    I tried to convince her that the police station was a mere mile away on this very road, but she would have none of it. For Debbie it was a matter of courage, plain and simple…But wait, what's that in the distance…ah a police cruiser. I gave Debbie a triumphant glare.

    But what was it about her? Even though she was ticking me off. I liked her right from the beginning. Hmm, was it because she was a fellow Leo?

On some level, that very first evening, something clicked between us. When it's two people of the opposite sex, it's called "chemistry." Who could have known that night, Debbie would end up being my soul mate.

When I was fifteen, and I was having a hard time (like many teenagers but a little more intense), I decided to do the sane, responsible thing—I decided to run away. Of course I called Debbie to tell her. She met me at Mr. Pizza in East Brunswick. Kept me there through a couple of slices of pizza. Asking questions, not really passing judgment on my answers, or lack thereof. Finally, it was time to go, don't ask me where. I was clueless. She convinced me to come to her house "for dinner, or at least a little snack." I agreed and stayed for five months. Throughout those five months we shared a room. She shared her room with me and she never complained. Well she did complain, but in a sisterly "you're getting on my nerves" sort of way. We both did. There was laughter, there were tears, there were parties. What probably sticks with me the most are the conversations we had just before we would fall asleep, with the lights out. Sharing secret dreams, fears and pieces of our hearts chunks of our souls. Finding out the most annoying little things about each other. Like college roommates—no, wait, actually more like being married! I find myself smiling now at the very thought.

When I came to live with Debbie and her dad, I remember when he came home we were sitting in the living room. Debbie had said to me, come back to my house and stay with me – I said O.K., I didn't have anything with me (that little con artist). Debbie's dad was working in the prisons. He hadn't come home from work yet. We were waiting and it was getting dark soon and I thought I should leave and Debbie kept coming up with these stupid things like, maybe we should write down a plan as to where you should go. Maybe we should do this or that, and I realized she was really stalling for time.

Then her daddy came home and there was Debbie with that little smile, you know, that Debbie smile. Well, "Daddy, Eileen was going to run away and blah, blah, blah and Daddy this and Daddy that." And guess what, Debbie's daddy, took me in for 5 months.

I remember one particular conversation with Debbie. It was the kind of a conversation you have with a person you know is dying. Debbie and I had talked quite a bit and had some really personal, intimate conversations during her final months. (One thing I admired about Debbie was that she only expressed regrets about things she hadn't done, not about anything she had actually accomplished.) Anyway, we were having a conversation and she told me that the only thing about dying that was frightening and upsetting was the fact that she "hadn't left her mark on the world." Those were her exact words. She regretted that she didn't have a child. Yes, a child to love and be loved unconditionally, but even more importantly, a way to leave her mark, a way to say to the world, "Hey, I was here and here's the living, breathing proof." Well, I started to cry. I told her that it wasn't true, that she had left her mark. *I* was her mark. *I* was the living, breathing proof that Debbie Liss was here. We both cried. You know the expression, "There but for the grace of God go I." Well, not to be blasphemous, but I could amend it "there but for the grace of God and Debbie go I." It was a very special moment between us. One I wish would have never come about, under those circumstances.

It is something I do believe in my heart. *I* am her mark. Debbie touched me and affected my life, just as she touched everyone who knew her.

First Legal Drink

Debbie turned eighteen on August 9, 1977 and was preparing to leave for college at the University of Washington. Before she did, she wanted to spend a day with her father, her "Daddy." Again, I refer to myself in this book as "Daddy," because she never referred to me in any other terms from the time she was a baby to the time she left this earth, I was always her "Daddy." One of the most painful parts of losing her is that I'll never hear her say the word "Daddy" again. There is a great amount of pain associated with never hearing that word from Debbie.

You know, when we talk about firsts—and this is going to be a story about her first legal drink—I want to mention that throughout her life Debbie would always be the first to call me and wish me a Happy Birthday and a Happy Father's Day, regardless of what time of day or evening it was. When she moved to Israel (there is a 7 hour time difference between the two countries), at one minute after 12 on September 2, she would call me making sure she was the first of all the children to wish me happy birthday. She also was the first of my children to send me flowers on my birthday. When you lose a child, there are many things that you lose, little things like the phone call on your birthday, the flowers, the word "Daddy," which will never be heard or received again from Debbie. These are the major parts of the great pain that every parent feels in that situation. We all have so many beautiful memories of our children and also such great pain over the loss of our child. It is really the little things in life that are important.

Now, to return to the subject of this chapter, When Debbie turned eighteen, she said, "I want you to buy me my first legal drink and I would love to have it at Freehold Racetrack." That was a great place to buy a first drink, since Debbie also loved to gamble. Debbie loved going to Freehold, which is a harness racing track in New Jersey. When she and I went to the track, we didn't go outside and sit on a bridge chair, or in the grandstand, we went to the restaurant and had lunch or dinner while watching the races, and that was true whether we went to Freehold or the Meadowlands. Debbie loved to be treated in style. She loved living the good life and, by the way, there is nothing wrong with that.

I took the day off from work and Debbie and I, just the two of us, went to Freehold Racetrack. We sat in the restaurant watching the races. She wanted to do the ordering and that is where she ordered her first legal drink.

It would be almost four months before I saw Debbie again, but the memory of sharing her first legal drink with me signifying, "I am now legally an adult" would be with me forever.

Cheaper To Grow It Than To Buy It

When Debbie was 18, she had graduated East Brunswick High School and had been accepted to the University of Hartford in Connecticut and was ready to attend school there. But now—back tracking a little—another party comes into play here and his name is David. David and Debbie were an item from the time Debbie was 16; I think David was a year or two older. For two years they went steady and were supposedly very much in love. Debbie was focusing on a career and thinking about teaching or working in some capacity with children. She wanted to go to college, and of course I encouraged her and supported this decision.

She had been accepted and was registered at the University of Hartford and everything was set for her to attend school in September 1977. But when David found out that Debbie was going to Hartford, he went and got an apartment nearby, in order to be near to her. I realized that she could not focus on her education if David was going to be close by; it was Debbie's feeling also that she should go as far away as possible from David, since she really wanted to get an education.

"Daddy," she says, "you've got to get me into another college and make sure it is far away from the East Coast because I think my relationship with David would interfere with my college." And of course I wholeheartedly agreed with her. At that time, I happened to have a friend who had connections with the University of Washington in Seattle. He was a former graduate of the University of Washington, who also had obtained his doctorate there and currently had two of his children attending the school. He was confident, that with Debbie's credentials, her good high school grades, he could get her into the University of Washington. Now that is pretty far away—I mean Seattle, Washington. You can't get much further away from New Jersey.

By August 1977, Debbie was enrolled as a student at the University of Washington. Well, guess what—no sooner was Debbie enrolled at the

University of Washington than David moved to Santa Monica, California, where, I believe, he had an uncle who was going to get him a job somewhere. David now began to call Debbie almost nightly, telling her how much he misses her, and why doesn't she join him? Santa Monica is beautiful, it is right near the ocean, and they could have this great life and the only reason she is in college is to please her father and she really doesn't need a college education. Adding the fact that she was lonely and homesick to David's nightly phone calls…by November, Debbie had had it. She decided to drop out of college, come home and take a look at her life. While David is making these phone calls and telling her about how much he misses her, he becomes involved with another woman. Debbie does not know what is going on in Santa Monica and she comes home around Thanksgiving and says, "Daddy, I need to look at my life. I have no idea what I want to do but I do feel I want to spend more time with Dave." Meanwhile, I have found out what I've just reported—that David now has two women. He is coming home for Christmas to be with his family and is then going to decide which of these two women, Debbie or this other person, will be his choice to bring back to Santa Monica!

    I said to Debbie, "Why are you throwing your life away, you should be in college, if you can't make it in Washington, we will find some other school, wherever it is, but please do not get trapped into this situation with Dave." But of course, at 18, Debbie is not listening to her father so—guess what, Debbie wins the lottery—Dave chooses Debbie over the other person. And soon enough, in January, 1978, at age 18 1/2, Debbie and David move to California and become a pair. Now, finally to the title of this chapter, "Cheaper To Grow It Than To Buy It."

    For the next six months the relationship between Debbie and me was pretty strained. I informed her that I would not support them, that if they wanted to be partners then they would have to support each other. If she decided to go back to school I would certainly support her and pay for her room and board, etc. Debbie obtained a job at an insurance company and David was working somewhere else. They bought a car, furniture and they were living together and that is where it was. In the summer of 1978, I wanted to go to Santa Monica for Debbie's nineteenth birthday on August 9. I had not seen her in over 6 months and even though I did not support their lifestyle, I still loved my daughter very much, missed her and I still hoped that eventually she would see the light and leave this relationship. Until then, I wanted to see her and spend some time with her.

So I went to California for her 19th birthday. They had a pretty nice apartment, bedroom, living room, and I noticed that they had a little porch outside. I had stopped smoking for a year, even though it was very difficult—even more difficult when I am sitting in a room and I am seeing Debbie and Dave smoking. I decided to get some fresh air out on the porch. Well, Debbie and David said, "you don't really want to go out on the porch, please don't go out on the porch." I didn't understand why I couldn't go out on the porch—they were very forceful in trying to prevent me from going out on the porch and the more they were, the more I wanted to go out on the porch. When I finally went out on the porch, I immediately saw why. There, in large pots, was marijuana growing on the porch. It is illegal to own it, it is illegal to smoke it, and here they are growing marijuana plants. I mean, I was— "Debbie what is going on here, what is this stuff?" Debbie replies, "In our generation we smoke pot and all our friends and everybody else smokes pot and it is very expensive and we don't earn that much money so we found out it is *cheaper to grow it than to buy it.*" With that I grabbed one of her cigarettes and said, "well I can't take this any more" and I put a cigarette in my mouth. Debbie says, "Daddy, you quit for a whole year," and I said, "it is also cheaper to smoke regular cigarettes than to smoke pot."

Well, I don't blame Debbie for my going back to smoking at that time but that was 1978 and I didn't quit smoking until 1983. I guess it was "cheaper to grow it than to buy it."

David's Stories

Debbie was the most beautiful person ever to come into my life. She was of strong mind, yet sensitive and caring. I consider myself a better person for having known her.

The first time I met Debbie was on a blind date. I was seventeen years old and engaged to be married. Debbie cut school and I picked her up for the day. We spent the day talking about our deepest and most personal feelings. It was as though I was being honest with myself for the first time in my life. Debbie was a good listener. She opened her heart for me that day. We shared dreams and hopes of what might be, and cried about things we could not change.

I fell in love that day. I wanted nothing less than to be Debbie's "Knight in Shining Armor." It was not until many years later that I realized Debbie was my angel on earth, without whom I might not be here today.

Throughout our relationship, music played a significant role in both our lives. It was our favorite form of entertainment. We rarely went anywhere without our guitars. All our friends would get together at the beach, a park, or at someone's home to play music and sing songs. Debbie was a little shy, unless we were with close friends. I'll always remember one special song she would play and sing for me. It was a beautiful love song. I can still picture her as she looked into my eyes and played with such feeling and emotion. It will always remind me of her. The song was, "As Tears Go By," by the Rolling Stones.

One night I wrote a song for Debbie. I couldn't wait for her to hear it. We didn't have a phone, so my friend Bill and I drove to the local Seven-Eleven store which had a pay phone. I had taken my guitar with me. It was after midnight, but Debbie had a phone in her room. I called and woke her up and sang the song over the phone, accompanied on my guitar. My love song to her was called "Without You."

Many years later during a very difficult time in my life, I found Debbie still living in Santa Monica, California. I surprised Debbie with a visit. She was living with a girlfriend. After we talked a while and caught up on things going on in our lives, Debbie went to her room and brought out her guitar and an old sheet of music. It was the original copy of the love song I had written late one lonely night, all those years ago. I could hardly believe she had saved it all these years. I played and sang the song for her and her roommate. It was a very moving experience, one I will always cherish.

We talked all night, and many days to follow. It was though we were never apart. That was when I first realized how sick Debbie was. I had never heard of Lupus. I refused to accept that Debbie might never be well again.

Ethel's (David's Mother) Stories

I have a hard time putting into words what I feel in my heart, but I'll give you some of the "Debbie's Stories" I can remember.

I first met Debbie when she was a teenager, when she was dating my son David…but had the privilege of watching her grow into a smart, beautiful young lady, for although the relationship with my son did end, my relationship with Debbie never ended.

Once Debbie told me she went to a Catholic Church with her friends and wanted to receive communion, just like they did. How insulted she was when the priest refused. I don't know how the priest knew she was Jewish, but I can imagine the look on her girlfriends' faces and hers

Debbie's parents planned a trip to Europe one year, and Debbie got sick and needed a place to recuperate. She asked to stay at our home. I was honored that her parents trusted us. I enjoyed every minute of playing nursemaid and Debbie enjoyed the attention I very willingly gave her. I believe Debbie and David did some planning to make this all happen and had a few of their own ideas about recuperating.

To this day, I never cook and serve lamb chops without remembering it was Debbie's favorite meal. I tried to have it for her each time she came for a visit.

In November 1978, I made a trip out to California to visit David and Debbie. When I arrived, they said I would share a bedroom with Debbie, and David would take the couch. Now Debbie (and David was no better) never jumped out of bed when the alarm went off. It took at least five or six rings before either of them would move. I finally said, "I'll take the couch and you two can have the bedroom." They lived in a beautiful apartment, in a very nice area of Santa Monica, just a few blocks from the ocean. It seemed they were so busy working and going to school, they were never home very much to enjoy the area.

One Christmas, Debbie came to my house with a package of cookie-cutter ornaments made by a family child member. The child wasn't allowed to keep them so Debbie asked if I would put them on our Christmas tree, and I agreed. I had those ornaments until just a few years ago, when they started to fall apart.

On a very special Christmas, Debbie gave me a porcelain figure of the Blessed Virgin. It sits on my night stand to this day, and always reminds me of that Christmas.

I always had a very close relationship with Debbie. No matter what troubled Debbie, she would tell me about it. I couldn't always help, but I was a good listener and that was all she needed. We discussed everything, from loves, sicknesses, family disagreements, etc. I miss and love her very much.

Debbie Gives Daddy Permission

After about 2 years of the relationship with David, Debbie left at the age of 21, she moved in with one of her associates at Penncorp, who is also named Debbie. The apartment is on 3rd Street in Santa Monica, three blocks from the beach. Debbie would remain in this apartment for the balance of the time she was in California. It is in the same apartment building that her brother Jeff now lives with his wife Liz. They put a sign by each bedroom, Debbie 1 and Debbie 2. Debbie 2 is my daughter and Debbie 1 is this other young lady, whose apartment this was first. Just a tidbit, but Debbie Liss moved in with nothing, just the clothes on her back, after her relationship with David ended

It is now 1980 and Debbie has just been diagnosed with lupus (I will talk about her lupus in other chapters). During the Christmas holidays that year, 1980-81, I plan a trip to California to be with her, meet her new roommate and spend some quality time, a couple of weeks, with my daughter. Debbie had talked and written to me about how much she liked her roommate and her roommate's family. How Debbie 1's mother was like a mother to her out there and how close they became, especially now with the support she was getting with her lupus. Debbie was very anxious for me to meet them.

At this time, Debbie was in a relationship with a fellow by the name of Roy, and Debbie 1 was also in a relationship. Unbeknown to me—this will become very well known once I get out to California (Debbie is a plotter and schemer)—Debbie really wanted me to come out to California for other reasons as well. She knew that I wasn't that happy in my current relationship and she felt that this would be great thing—it would be a win-win. She would get me out of an unhappy relationship, and I would be happier. She would then have her father in California with all the support and love I could give her as she was combating this dreaded disease called lupus. One night, while in

California, she said to me, "Why don't we all go out—three couples." I said, "what do you mean three couples? I know you and Roy are a couple and Debbie 1 has her boyfriend, but what about me?" She said, "Well, why don't you go out with Debbie's mom, she's divorced and I want you to meet her anyway. Why don't we all go out to dinner and it would be nice." I said sure. I had nothing against going to dinner with Debbie's mom; she has been such a great support and had been there for Debbie, why not. The two Debbies had everything set up. They had Debbie's mom come over to meet me and have a little cocktail hour before we go out to dinner. She was a lovely woman, attractive, very congenial. We (now 3 couples) go out to the Chart House in Malibu. It's on the ocean and kind of a romantic place. During dinner, whenever Debbie had a chance to talk to me privately, she would ask, "Well, how do you like her? She's nice, I told you she was nice. Isn't she nice?"

I said, "Yes she is a very lovely woman, but you know I'm involved already, what are you getting at?"

"Just want to know if she is nice and I thought you would like her." We had a nice dinner, the two Debbies invite us all back to their place for an after-dinner drink. I believe this was on a Friday night so there was no work the next day for anyone and we could stay up later. We are sitting in their living room, the two girls are there with their boyfriends and I am sitting with Debbie 1's mom. At about 1 or 1:30 AM, Debbie 1's mom said, "I'm really tired, I think I am going to go home." I said, "Do you mind if I walk you down to your car," I thought that was being gentlemanly. In fact, I believe my daughter Debbie said, "Daddy why don't you walk her down to the car." I walked her to the car, told her how much I appreciated all the support she was giving Debbie, and how much Debbie needs that kind of support with her illness, and how Debbie felt she was like a mom to her. I said that I'd really had a nice evening. I think I gave her a hug and said thank you again and I went upstairs.

Well, when I came upstairs, my Debbie greeted me with: "What are you doing here?"

I said, "Well—I'm staying here with you—why did you ask me that?"

Debbie responds, "We set it all up so that the two of you could be together tonight at her mom's house."

I said, "Debbie what are you talking about?"—and then she said, and I will never forget the words, "Daddy, it is O.K. I give you permission to sleep with her."

I believe I responded, "Debbie, I really don't need permission if I wanted to but I don't want to. It was very nice of the two of you to set everything up and thank you." By the way, it never did work out the way the two Debbie's had planned but thank you, my daughter, for thinking of me.

Coping With An Incurable Disease

(written by Debbie while a student at Santa Monica Community College, 1982)

Systemic Lupus Erythematosus. Words I couldn't pronounce on sight. Words that had no meaning to me and sounded evil. After three months of numerous and various tests and four days following my twenty first birthday, those words became my reality. I had Systemic Lupus Erythematosus.

Systemic Lupus Erythematosus (S.L.E.), like leukemia and cancer, is an incurable disease that can kill. It is a disease that afflicts almost one million people and, for reasons that are unknown at this time, 90% of them are young women. S.L.E. lies in the category of arthritis because lupus is a "connective tissue disorder." But, in the last twenty years, research is zeroing in on the immune system. To make it very simple, our antibodies fight off the good cells in our body instead of the infectious ones. As it has been stated, "Lupus is the prototype, the classic and confounding example of what is perhaps the most perplexing puzzle in medicine (not including the aberrant cell proliferation of the cancers): the body actively, viciously mobilized against itself." It is this misdirection of our antibodies that can eventually kill.

Learning what S.L.E. is, was my first step in dealing with the monster that was eating me up alive. I had to know what lupus was so I could start disproving my diagnosis. Denial, that was a good place to start with overcoming my misfortunes, or so I thought at the time. I did a good job of it too, until I realized that I couldn't prove the doctor wrong

Once the fact sunk in that I indeed had an incurable disease, I began feeling very sorry for myself. Why me? What have I done to deserve this? My doctor told me blatantly that I could either work or go to school, not both. I was advised not to drink, smoke, stay out late or do anything that tired me. He also told me to avoid any stress, since stress can cause you to flare-up. Not only was he telling me, a twenty-one year old to stop living, but I must live on drugs to control the disease and come every two weeks for blood and urine tests. How dare he, were my thoughts, then and for a while thereafter.

I began doing research on the drugs, and with my family's help, I found out some disturbing facts that the doctor neglected telling me. For example, the Plaquenil I was taking had proven side effects of irreversible damage to the retina to your eyes. That was the turning point for me. I stopped feeling sorry for myself and began looking at my options.

When dealing with a fact, such as an incurable disease that significantly affects one's life, each and everyone of us finds a way not to deal with it. I did, but with time and help from family, friends and professionals, I learned how to cope. I took a step forward and learned about my body, my mind, the value of human life, what to do and what not to do to keep myself from a flare-up. I haven't seen a doctor in over two and a half years. And with any luck, I will stay in remission for years. I'm a stronger person now than I was at age twenty one, and I can say with much confidence in my voice, "I have Systemic Lupus Erythematosus and I am going to live."

Las Vegas

Debbie and a girlfriend, Shannon, who also worked with her at Penncorp, loved to go to Las Vegas. Vegas is maybe 5 hours driving time from the Los Angeles area. They would go approximately once a month and spend a weekend there, enjoying the tables. Debbie loved the Vegas atmosphere; in fact, she referred to Vegas as "Adult Disneyland." Debbie and Shannon would go to the Riviera Hotel, which was their favorite, and I think they became friends with one of the dealers or croupiers, who arranged to get them special discounts on meals, rooms, etc. It was known about Penncorp that both Debbie and Shannon had friends in Vegas and they loved going there. So once a month, on a Friday afternoon, they would take off and head to Vegas. This story relates to one of those weekends.

On this particular Friday, just before she left, Debbie's boss called her in and said to Debbie, "Here is $10.00, and this is what I want you do. Either tonight or tomorrow night, when you get to the craps table (make sure it is late at night), when you are rolling the dice, I want you to put the 10 bucks on the come line, then roll and if you win I want you to keep the amount going and going for eight times. If you lose then you lose, if you win just keep on rolling," and those were his instructions. (I am not a craps player, so I don't know what most of that means.)

Debbie and Shannon leave for Vegas, get to the Riviera and do their thing. I believe it was Saturday night, they were playing craps and it was late at night, 2:00 or 3:00 in the morning, when it is now Debbie's turn to roll the dice. I don't know how many people were around at that time, but Debbie announces to the group around the table that she is putting $10.00 on the come line and that it is for her boss and that if she makes the point, she is going to keep on rolling and continue with the amount she is winning for 8 times. If she craps out then the money is gone but if she wins she will continue for the 8 times. Well, half the people by this time are pretty happy and they said we will join you and they each put $10.00 down on the come line. Now she has a big fan club rooting for her as she rolls the dice. The first roll, and she is a winner, now she has got $20.00

down. Then she rolls again and she is a winner, and now she has $40.00 down. She goes the third time, she rolls it and she is a winner. We are going to roll this thing to $40, 80, 160, 320, 640, 1,280, it went up to $2,560.00. The last time she rolled it and won, she won $2,560.00. Well, the whole place is going wild, but that small group that started out with her, each one of them won $2,560.00 also. Then she just throws the dice away, because that was the commitment, she takes her chips and she and Shannon go to the cashier and cash in.

On Monday morning Debbie reports to work and of course the boss is anxious to find out what happened to his $10.00. Just to show you how honest she is—remember, the boss has no clue as to what happened; she could have walked in and said, "Hey boss, I rolled the dice, I lost, you lost your 10 bucks." But she has $2,560.00 in her purse, and she walks in and he says," Good morning—so how did you do?" Debbie takes out the $2,560.00; she gives it all to him and says, "Here! You are a winner, we won $2,560.00 for you."

Well, you can imagine how this guy felt. Honesty is still the best policy and it did pay off. He said to Debbie, "You know, you are a winner, too," and he gave her $500.00 and said thank you. Well, what would you have done?

Toni's Stories

I met Debbie in the summer of 1979. We both worked on the executive floor of a company in Santa Monica. Debbie was very outgoing and easy to know, so it was only a short time before we became friends. We would go to lunch almost daily, a couple of days a week to our favorite Chinese restaurant, then after work for "happy hour" at "Apples" located down the street from our office. Chicken wings and zucchini sticks were Debbie's favorites!

Our friendship grew rather quickly and was unique in the sense that we just seemed to hear and understand each other and could be ourselves without any pretense or fear of being judged. We found that we were very much alike, yet respected one another's differences.

I learned of her Lupus early on and always supported the restrictions she was faced with every day. She would never complain or dwell on it nor would she allow that to be a burden to herself or others. It was remarkable how she managed to look at each day as a new beginning even without knowing what the next day would hold for her.

Debbie was really interested in hockey (California Kings now the Los Angeles Kings) and of course, baseball's New York Mets. We would have a lot of fun going to the games, sometimes rooting for the opposing teams. It didn't matter though, as the celebration would always be the same!

Debbie also enjoyed ice skating and, at times, I would go watch her skate. She was quite the skater, and even though sometime she didn't feel her best, that wouldn't stop her! She liked to keep active and really enjoyed going out and having fun. She loved to laugh and had a great sense of humor. Her charming wit drew the attention of many around her which made it easy for her to make friends.

Since Debbie lived by the beach, we would spend time down on Main Street, Santa Monica. Again, another place to get those chicken wings and zucchini sticks. After lunch, we would go back to her place and sit and talk for hours. We never would run out of things to talk, laugh or even cry about.

We also went on a few trips together. Two of them we both remembered fondly and talked about frequently, Big Bear Mountain and Las Vegas. Like the time at Big Bear Mountain and we went out walking, enjoying the fresh air. In the hills, at a close distance, we could see coyote eyes staring at us. It really caught us off guard and needless to say, we cut our walk short. That story was talked about for years.

Then on our flight to Las Vegas, we had a little scare because of the way the pilot was flying the plane. We weren't sure if it was due to turbulence or just that he couldn't fly the plane very well. It wouldn't have been so bad except that our imaginations got the best of us when the pilot, for some reason, asked for a spoon over the intercom. For some bizarre reason, we found that quite funny.

During the mid 1980's, I sang karaoke at a local nightclub. Debbie was one of my main supporters and would come regularly to listen to me sing. One of her favorite songs was the "Theme From Ice Castles," so I would make sure I sang that for her every night she came.

Then, after a few years, Debbie moved away, first back to New Jersey, then on to Israel. It was very difficult to see her move away, but even with the miles between us, we continued to stay close and always were working on a plan for the next time we would meet. I had hoped one day to get to Israel, but sadly, that didn't happen!

As I close, I recall a few words from Debbie's favorite song, "Ice Castles." "And now I do believe that even in a storm we'll find some light." This song will always remind me of Debbie and the positive outlook she had on life. I so admired her for the inner strength and courage she displayed while she struggled with the many obstacles she faced in her life.

Debbie looked forward each day with deep affection and love from within her heart. And her family and friends were an added lifeline to her soul. I was truly blessed to have been part of that lifeline and to have shared all that she was and all that she hoped to be.

Our friendship was very meaningful, filled with so many special memories, and I truly miss her as I hold dear to my heart these memories and more. With love in my heart, I will always remember fondly the beautiful difference she made in my life.

It has been a privilege and an honor to share these memories for this special tribute!

With Love and Friendship,

Toni

Opening Day at Shea

During Debbie's lifetime, I attended Opening Day at Shea Stadium only once. It was in the mid-eighties, when Debbie was still living in California. However, even though she wasn't at the game with me, she was most definitely a part of this opening day story.

The year was 1985, the Mets had just obtained Gary Carter from the Montreal Expos and he became a very important part of both opening day and this story. I came to the game very early since I wanted to be a part of all the festivities, my first opening day. As I was walking outside the ballpark that morning, I noticed a crowd gathering around a T.V. cameraman. Being curious, I walked over to them to see what was happening. It was a local New York, channel 4 cameraman and newscaster asking fans their opinions of the Mets' chances of winning the pennant. As I got closer to the newscaster, he spotted me and asked me to come forward to be interviewed. Wow, I thought, not only was I going to attend my first opening day game, but now I was going to be on T.V. as well. He asked me the same question he was asking these young people, what was my opinion of the Mets chances of winning the pennant this year? Before I volunteered an answer, I said, "May I first say hello to my daughter Debbie in California?" "California," he said, This is Channel Four, in New York City, we don't reach California, only the greater New York Metropolitan Area." Well, I felt pretty foolish. I proceeded to give him a very lengthy perspective of the Mets chances how with the addition of Gary Carter, our great pitching staff, etc., we should definitely be contenders for the pennant.

It was really a very exciting game that even went into extra innings, and had a story book finish, Gary Carter, the newest Met, steps up to the plate in the bottom of the 10th inning and hits his first home run as a Met, to win the ballgame.

I couldn't wait to get home, call California and tell Debbie all the happenings of my first opening day at Shea. She knew that I was attending the game, but unknown to me, she was also taping the game so that she could see it when she came home from work that evening. (At that time,

Channel 9, WWOR-TV telecast most of the Mets home games, and like a "super station," was picked up by cable systems all over the country.) I arrived home about 5:30 PM (2:30 PM California time), called Debbie and left this very long message on her answering machine. How I was interviewed by Channel Four, before the game, telling them I wanted to say hello to my daughter Debbie in California, how they told me, politely, how stupid I was to think that this interview would ever be seen in California, etc. Then, I proceeded to tell Debbie all about the game including how Gary Carter hit a home run and won the game in the bottom of the 10th inning.

Now, Debbie having taped the game, at about 5:30 PM her time, opens the door to her apartment. She immediately sits down and starts viewing the tape of the ballgame. After about three or four innings of the game, she decided to check her messages. Guess what, my long message begins to play. When she realizes that I am about to tell her how this exciting game is going to end, she stops the message, picks up the phone, and dials her daddy back in New Jersey. I can remember that phone call as if it were yesterday. "Daddy," she screamed into the phone, "don't you know that I taped the entire game and here you are telling me on the phone how it ended. I don't want to know how it ends! I want to see it for myself, that's why I taped the game! You're going to spoil it for me." I apologized and asked her, "how many innings have you seen?" Three or four, she replied, and I said, "well, I won't tell you who won or anything, except that you will be happy with the ending."

"Daddy", she said, "you just spoiled it for me anyway."

"No," I said, "you still have to see the entire game to know it ended happily."

We both laughed, said how much we loved each other and that's how my first opening day at Shea ended.

It Will Hurt You More Than It Will Hurt Me

When Debbie was diagnosed with lupus, she was living in California (during the period from 1980 to 1989). Debbie used many excellent coping methods and treatment therapies that we would call today "alternative" or "holistic" therapies. She held a full time job at Penncorp, an insurance company, and at the same was able to attend evening classes at Santa Monica Community College. Debbie completed her Associate's Degree in Business during that period of time, which, while dealing with her illnesses, and especially given the fact that she was afflicted with both lupus and scleroderma, was really a great achievement. To hold a full time job, go to school in the evening and complete a degree program, while she was also participating in a number of treatment modalities, was truly amazing and an outstanding accomplishment.

Lupus is an autoimmune disease without a known cause or cure. There are different treatment modalities that have met with some success, including drug therapy as well as the route that Debbie took, which was alternative medicine. One of her main symptoms, and the one most common lupus and scleroderma patients experience, is fatigue and joint pain, closely related to rheumatoid arthritis. She also had "Raynaud's Syndrome," a circulatory condition affecting her extremities These pains are not just the average "run of the mill" pains, but pains that are so great, that in many cases could incapacitate an individual. It was recommended to Debbie that an acupuncturist might help her with both her Raynaud's as well as relieve some of her pain. She began acupuncture and went two to three times a week.

It was while on one of my frequent visits to California following her diagnosis that Debbie asked me to attend an acupuncture session with her so that I could observe her treatment.

I will always remember that afternoon when we visited her acupuncturist. I sat down in the room where she was going to receive her needles. The doctor indicated to me exactly what was going to happen and explained also the theory of acupuncture and how this was an old Chinese treatment that has been very successful in relieving pain. One of the main goals and purposes of the program with Debbie was to relieve some of the pain associated with her lupus/scleroderma, as well as improve her circulation.

As the doctor began inserting needles, first to her head and forehead and then placing needles throughout different points of her body, I said, "Hold it—doesn't it hurt?" I had never seen acupuncture performed before, even though I had heard very favorable reports from those who had received it, especially from Debbie. Debbie said, and I quote, "Daddy, this is going to hurt you more than it hurts me." How right she was. I was literally experiencing the pain that I thought she was experiencing every time a needle was stuck in a part of her body. Fortunately, it was not actually painful at all and, in fact, she laughed as he inserted needle after needle. This entire process lasted about 45 minutes and then the needles were removed. Debbie felt great.

As footnote to this, a few years later I developed a chronic back problem and remembered Debbie recommending that I go to an acupuncturist. I did attend acupuncture for about 3 sessions. Unfortunately, it was not helpful for me. Still, I can attest that the needles did not hurt one bit. In fact, while I was lying on the table and the needles were being inserted I felt good and that good feeling lasted for half an hour after the treatment.

But finally, I will never forget Debbie saying, "This will hurt you more than it hurts me."

Baseball

Debbie was a big sports fan. She loved all sports. In fact, I believe that Debbie could have been one of the first women sportscasters had she pursued that career, rather than going into the insurance field. She not only loved baseball, football, basketball and hockey, she was also a great fan of the New York teams, the Mets, the Knicks, the Giants and the Rangers. She could tell you the batting averages of every Mets batter, the ERAs, of every Mets pitcher. She could tell you how many points each hockey player had and how many goals scored and who the leading basketball scorers were for the Knicks. She was extremely knowledgeable and she took her sports very seriously. She and her friend Shannon, who was a huge San Francisco Giants fan, would follow their teams religiously. Debbie and Shannon each had their favorite players as well. Shannon was a big Jack Clark fan, and Debbie a big Keith Hernandez fan. Actually Debbie's fantasy was to have a relationship with Keith that would eventually lead to marriage, a real fantasy. Besides having their own idols, they really loved baseball and their respective teams.

On their West Coast trips, the Mets would go to San Francisco to play the Giants 3 games, then go to Los Angeles to play the Dodgers and then on down to San Diego to play the Padres. They would normally do this West Coast trip twice a year. Shannon and Debbie would take vacation days to coincide with the Mets' California trips. San Francisco was a 400-mile trip for them, so when the Mets came out to San Francisco, they had to take 3 days off. In L.A. they didn't have to take time off because they lived right outside L.A. In San Diego, it would depend on whether it was a weekend or not if they needed time off from work. But regardless, when the Mets came to California, Debbie and Shannon would not only spend their vacation time with them, but would make sure they stayed in the same hotel with the ballplayers. They wanted to get as close to these players as possible.

Now you have the picture ... these two girls, Debbie and Shannon, not only close friends and gambling partners but baseball fanatics. That's exactly where the term *fan* comes from and that's what they were: FAN-ATICS.

This is a story concerning a weekend when the Mets were playing in San Diego. It was a Saturday night and after the game both Debbie and Shannon went back to the hotel and directly to the lounge. There, lo and behold, were some of the Mets T.V.announcers, Tim McCarver being one of them. Debbie goes over to Tim, introduces herself and goes on to tell him that she is a BIG Mets fan, travels up and down the coast to see the Mets—and how her father is an even bigger Mets fan living back in the New York area. She then asks Tim, would he be kind enough to make an announcement during Sunday's Mets—Padres game, something like—"Hi, Dad, this is from Debbie, just wanted to say hi, I love you and miss you.". Well, Tim was very gracious and said sure he would. Debbie writes everything down and gives it to Tim and is very excited that her name and my name would be linked forever on T.V. She was going to make this a big surprise so she never called to tell me that I should watch Sunday's game and that my name and her name are going to be "all over the country. "

As it happened, that Sunday I was involved in a charity fund raiser, which was a bus ride to Atlantic City. I therefore was not going to be home, and thus would not be watching the Mets game. Well, sometime during that afternoon, just as Tim McCarver promised, he indicated that he had a message from Debbie Liss to her father Moe Liss and the message was, "Hi! Just want you to know I'm thinking of you, I miss you, I love you, Debbie." Of course, the entire east coast, that was watching the Mets game, heard the message, including some of my friends and relatives—who immediately called my home. When I arrived home that Sunday evening there were numerous blinks on my answering machine. It was family and friends telling me how wonderful it was and "Where were you, did you see and hear the message?"

Well, I get on the phone and called California but I get Debbie's answering machine since she is still in San Diego. I say, "Hey, Debbie what is going on? I understand that my name was on T.V. this afternoon and you sent me a great message. I wasn't aware that you did this, but I want to thank you, call me when you get in." Around midnight the phone rings and it is Debbie, saying "Where were you? Here I am setting things up for you and you are not even around."

"Well, Debbie, I was in Atlantic City on a fundraiser and I didn't see it."

"Who gave you permission to go to A.C." (That's my daughter Debbie.)

"Why weren't you home watching the Mets game, where you should have been, because we needed you, because we lost" and so on and so on and so on That is my beautiful and loving daughter, always thinking of me, and that is another one of the Debbie's Stories I will never forget.

I mentioned earlier that both Debbie and Shannon had their favorites. Jack Clark, a power hitter for the San Francisco Giants, was Shannon's idol. Keith Hernandez was more than Debbie's idol; in fact Debbie kept reminding me, that with all my connections (whatever they were I didn't know any of them), that I should be able to "fix up" Debbie with Keith Hernandez. Invariably, whenever I went to a ball game she would say, "Well, I want you to get a message to Keith, I want you to see Keith, I want you to tell him that there is a big Mets fan out there who is in love with him." This went on for a few years and then one time, when I was on a business trip to St. Louis, it just happened that the Mets were in town to play the Cardinals. Keith Hernandez had been traded away from the Cardinals to the Mets and of course whenever you are traded away from a team, when you return to play that team, you really want to show them that they made a mistake. Keith was a big part of the Mets' success during the 80s, especially when they won the pennant and World Series in 1986. Debbie knew that I was in St. Louis and she decided this was her big moment. She figured that while I was in St. Louis I should look up Keith and in some way get to meet him. The least I could do was to fix him up with Debbie. I told Debbie, I will try to get to a game and get a message to him with your phone number on it. That was Plan B—not so bad, and she agreed to it. The message would read: "Hi Keith, my name is Debbie Liss I am a big fan of yours and would like to meet you. My phone number is ____ I live in Santa Monica, California and the next time you come out to California to play the Dodgers, please call me and let's get together." I wrote this out on a nice piece of paper, placed it in an envelope, and now here I'm at the Mets/Cardinal game. I was able to get seats down in the lower tier and, now saying to myself, How am I going to get this message to Keith? I'm thinking, if I can get down where the bullpen is, maybe I can get the attention of one of the relief pitchers, give him the message, and tell him it is for Keith Hernandez. Maybe he will give it to Keith. Maybe Keith will read it and maybe, and maybe and maybe. That was my plan of action. I gave the usher a few dollars so that he would let me go down to the railing near the field. Of course there are a lot of "kookies" out there who bother baseball players and it looked as though I was one of those "kookies", because I yelled out to one of the pitchers and said, "Can you do me a favor, my daughter is a big Mets fan and has a message she would like you to give to Keith Hernandez." He just ignored me but I was very persistent. I said, "Really it is very important that I get this message to Keith." Finally I convinced him and handed him the message which was in an envelope addressed to Keith Hernandez.

I thought, I finally succeeded! I'll probably be at a wedding in a few years with my daughter and Keith. What happened to that message? I will never know. Unhappily, when the Mets went out to California the next time, Debbie didn't receive a phone call from Keith Hernandez. She never met Keith Hernandez and therefore she never married Keith Hernandez. To this day, every time I see or hear or read about Keith Hernandez I always remember that incident when I gave this letter to one of the Mets relief pitchers to give to Keith—and you know, to this day Debbie blames me for never fixing her up with Keith Hernandez. That is one of the biggest blemishes on my record in Debbie's eyes— never getting her fixed up with Keith"…..

Lupus Convention 1987, Chicago, Illinois (or, "Hi Daddy, I'm Here")

In 1987 both Debbie and I were very involved with the Lupus Foundation of America. We both held very responsible positions in our respective chapters that year. Debbie had been elected vice president of the Los Angeles Chapter, and I was the vice president of the New Jersey Chapter.

Every year the Lupus Foundation of America conducts a week-long national convention where representatives of chapters throughout the country meet to discuss the latest treatments and coping strategies, research results, news on lupus from the medical profession and other related health issues. That year, 1987, the convention was held in Chicago, during the month of July. Both Debbie and I were selected as delegates from our respective chapters. In addition to being a delegate, I was also a presenter at one of the numerous workshops that were conducted at the convention. As a teacher, trainer, facilitator and behavioral scientist I had performed a great amount of work in stress management over the years and especially on managing the stress of the chronically ill. I had conducted workshops for our local branches throughout New Jersey so now I was invited by the National Convention to present such a workshop in Chicago.

There were many sessions running concurrently for the 300 to 400 representatives at this convention but I will never forget this particular session. I was in the middle of my presentation, standing before 40 or 50 participants, when into the room walked my daughter Debbie. Without blinking an eyelash and saying any other words, I heard shouted "Hi Daddy, I'm here," and so Debbie, my daughter, made her grand entrance into my stress workshop. You talk about stress! Well, I guess you can say that my stress level increased a little bit at that moment. However, it provided a great moment of laughter and humor for the entire session, so in actuality, it was a great stress reliever for everyone in the room, except me of course. I then introduced my daughter and spent a few minutes talking about her, welcomed her and her friends to the workshop, and without missing a beat, continued dealing with stress and lupus.

Fighting For The Rights of Lupus Patients

This story takes place over the period 1987 to 1991. It is a story about Debbie's wrongful dismissal from the company that she had worked for 9-1/2 years, and the resulting battle between Debbie Liss and this big insurance company, Penncorp; the ultimate victory of Debbie not only for herself but for the rights of all lupus patients, and for that matter for all the chronically ill who are wrongfully dismissed and treated like second-class citizens.

First, a background to this story. Originally Debbie was diagnosed in 1980 with lupus, and she was treated for that disease, which is one of many closely related auto-immune diseases. It was six years later, while she was visiting me in New Jersey, that we made an appointment with one of the top lupus/scleroderma specialists in New York City. This was in 1986 when Debbie was really feeling very poorly. Lupus is a very up-and-down disease, with periods of remission when you are feeling very good, and periods of "flare" when, in many cases, you can't leave your home or even your bed. When Debbie and I entered the waiting room, there were about 20 to 30 people already there. This doctor, who had never seen Debbie but had copies of her records, eventually spent about twenty minutes with her. Following her exam, we both went into his office for a consultation. It was at that time that the doctor said, " Debbie, you don't have lupus; you have scleroderma." Scleroderma is a sister disease of lupus, another auto-immune disease, whose name literally translated is "hardening of the skin" For the next few years, we received similar diagnosis from other doctors. A renowned specialist associated with Robert Wood Johnson Medical Center, confirmed the diagnosis and when she returned to Israel, a rheumatologist recommended by a lupus specialist of Robert Wood Johnson Medical Center, also concurred that in fact what she had was scleroderma. My own feeling—I have been involved with lupus, working on a volunteer basis with lupus patients for 20 years—it is my strong feeling that she had over-lap, both lupus and scleroderma, which some people refer to as mixed connective tissue disease. I believe she had them both and since they are so closely related, it is very difficult to distinguish between the two.

With her coping mechanisms, primarily her holistic approach, mind-body activity, acupuncture, biofeedback, Debbie was able to complete her Associate Degree while working full time at Penncorp. This, however, took a toll on her, and by 1987 her illness was in a flare and she was unable to work full time. In fact, it was during this period of time that her brother Jeff moved out to California to be with her and be of assistance and support.

It was a very difficult time in her struggle with lupus/scleroderma. What made it even more difficult was that in order to support herself, she had to go on disability, leave her job, even though it was going to be, and this was clearly understood by all concerned, temporarily. She had an excellent work record at Penncorp and had been promoted to positions of responsibility in the company during her 9 1/2 year work history. She knew this disability would be a temporary situation until she could get her strength back and return to work. Everyone at Penncorp, including her supervisor, senior people as well as all her colleagues and friends, knew this was just a temporary setback. They all knew and understood, that she would regain her strength and energy and she would then return to her position.

It should be noted that Penncorp was a large insurance company, and self-insured all its employees. During this period of her illness, the various medical bills that Debbie incurred were paid by Penncorp, and that would be hundreds of thousands of dollars. They fought very hard to deny benefits for both her acupuncture and biofeedback, but they finally, under pressure, began to assume those bills as well. They originally felt these were not acceptable medical practices. However, when we were able to prove to Penncorp that there was no "cure" for lupus/scleroderma and that her doctors had recommended these treatments, they became eligible for reimbursement.

It should be noted also that once she had completed her tenth year with Penncorp, they would have to assume her pension as well – after ten years in the company you were eligible for pension and benefits. That is the picture at this point in her life when she went on disability and left work on a temporary basis.

After 6 months on disability, with rest and treatment, Debbie felt she was ready to return to work. She made an appointment with her supervisor, met with him and he then informed Debbie, that her position had been abolished. Not her work—that had been redistributed—but there was no position for her at Penncorp. Unfortunately, she was informed, you have been terminated from Penncorp. Everybody knew that this was illegal. One cannot be punished because one is on disability. Your job had to be maintained. And even if Debbie's job was abolished, her seniority of 9-1/2 years gave her the right to bump someone else with less seniority from a position. This was a fabrication, set up by the company for one main purpose — the bottom line was they wanted to save dollars. They knew that if they brought her back, not only would they in six months have to maintain a pension for her, but with her history of medical bills, they were aware that Debbie Liss working for Penncorp for the next 20 or 30 years probably meant millions of dollars in health benefits the company would have to absorb.

Debbie didn't take this laying down. After talking with me and with friends, colleagues, and her doctors, she decided to fight the insurance industry. Specifically, take Penncorp to court and have them own up to their responsibility. She was not just doing this for Debbie Liss, she was doing it for every lupus patient, for every chronically ill patient that had been treated this way by our insurance companies.

Debbie was fortunate in meeting a young lawyer who took her case on a contingency basis. The contingency was that whatever Debbie received, if she did receive an award by the court, he would receive a certain percentage. I met him, spent hours with him, he interviewed many other people who were involved with lupus, medical professionals, support group facilitators, etc., to build up this case and prove that not only could Debbie work, but that she was wrongfully dismissed and that we were fighting for the principle that chronically ill people cannot be treated this way.

The insurance company's plan was to delay, delay and delay. Of course, they never wanted this case to go to court. They didn't want to have a chronically ill young woman, taking the witness stand and addressing a jury who might well choose to beat down the insurance company. It was really a David and Goliath story, especially since the insurance company knew that they were wrong. So they kept delaying the court date hoping that either an out-of-court settlement would take place or Debbie would finally just drop the charges.

As we know, Debbie moved to Israel November, 1989, but the case continued with depositions being taken during her many visits to the states.

In 1991-92, a little more than four years after her dismissal and the actual filing of the suit, the case came to court. Debbie was told by her lawyer that the company would do everything in their power to destroy her credibility based on the fact that now she was in Israel, gainfully employed, and had no need of a position at Penncorp. Her lawyer was going to use this as an example for *her* case—that she was making a new life, able to learn a new language and obtain a new job demonstrated that she was able and capable of returning to work at Penncorp, and thus her dismissal was definitely wrongful.

A decision had to be made. Debbie knew she would have to take two to three weeks off from work in Israel to come to the States for the trial. She knew it would be hard and the stress might cause another flare. She had experienced a flare in the late 80s that had led to this problem in the first place, and she wasn't willing to sacrifice her health for whatever additional dollars, if it came before a jury. The insurance company probably was aware of this also, and so the company offered an out of court settlement. They really didn't want this to come to trial; they had delayed it for so many years because they did not want a jury of Debbie's peers to listen to the impact of this disease on Debbie's life, the pain and suffering she had experienced. They knew that a jury might award millions of dollars if the case went to trial.

The main purpose was not for Debbie to make a fortune out of this case. The main purpose was for her, on behalf of all the chronically ill people in this country, to stand up to the insurance companies and have them admit wrong-doing and then to have it published in the lupus news, medical journals and other periodicals, so that people are made aware that they can fight for their rights and win—that companies cannot wrongfully dismiss a person because of an illness.

An out of court settlement was made in favor of Debbie. She did receive a considerable amount— much, much less than what she would have received if she had gone to court. It was enough to pay her legal fees and for her to purchase a home in Israel.

The point of this story is that for four years Debbie became the champion of all those afflicted with lupus, scleroderma and any other chronic illness. She fought against the insurance industry and it was really a victory for the small people. I was so proud of her and it is something that everyone would be proud of—Debbie Liss's fight for justice.

Debbie, Pearl and My Mom

Let me preface this by saying that if it wasn't for Debbie, Pearl and I would have never met, fallen in love and become a very happily married couple. After Debbie was diagnosed with lupus, I made a commitment to her that I would spend the remainder of my life doing everything in my power to help her cope with this illness even if that meant leaving work and moving out to California to be with her, which at one time I did consider. (Eventually my son Jeff did move out to California in the late '80s, and lived with her. It was when Debbie was very ill. He is stilling living in California, with his wife Liz, in that same apartment complex that was once Debbie's.)

Anyway, getting back to the Pearl, Debbie and Mom story... because of my commitment to Debbie, I became very involved as a volunteer with the Lupus Foundation of New Jersey. Eventually I became an organizer of support groups, rap groups and branches throughout the state. By 1989, I became President of the Lupus Foundation of New Jersey. This is where Pearl gets involved. Pearl was the office manager for the Lupus Foundation of New Jersey during the period of time that I was active as a volunteer, and that is how the two of us met. Thus, we both have Debbie to thank, because if Debbie had not been diagnosed with lupus, I would have never been involved, would have never met Pearl and would never found the love of my life.

It was 1989 and Pearl and I were seeing each other. My mother was living in Florida; my father had passed away in 1980, the same year Debbie was diagnosed with Lupus—as you can imagine, that was a very difficult year for me. I wanted to visit my Mom, and since Debbie had made a decision to go to Israel later that year, this would also be an opportunity for her to see her Grandma, or as she affectionaately referred to her, "My Bubba," which is Grandma in Yiddish. I also thought this would be an opportunity for Pearl to meet my mother, since we were at that time thinking very seriously of becoming a pair and living together. We didn't want to shock my mother, because my mother didn't know anything about Pearl. So we conjured up a plan that the three of us would go to Florida to see my mother and present Pearl as Debbie's new girlfriend—a little older (there is an 11-year age difference in ages between Pearl and Debbie)—but that they were friends. The plan was to spend four or five days in Florida. We would be staying at a motel very close to the Century Village complex where my mother was living and would masquerade the fact that Pearl was Debbie's friend and Debbie wanted to say good-bye to her "bubba" and this was an opportunity for all of us to get together.

You can imagine how awkward the situation was as we were sitting in the living room of my mother's little condominium and representing Pearl to my mother as my daughter's close friend. Pearl was beautiful, warm and loving and my mother quickly liked her—how could she not. It was wonderful that she was such a nice friend, nice that you came down here, and so on. . However, Debbie felt very uneasy. "Daddy, how long are you going to keep this masquerade up? You know you have to tell Bubba sometime before we leave that this is not my close friend, this may be my future step-mom." Pearl also felt awkward with the situation. I figured it was about time. At first I thought I would tell my mom at breakfast, in the restaurant we normally went to. But Debbie said, "you know how hard of hearing Bubba is, you would be screaming this out. Do you want everyone in Florida to hear? Why not tell her at home." And once again Debbie was right on target. Later on that week we broke the news that Pearl and I were a pair and that this was not Debbie's close friend but could be Debbie's future step-mom.

The response from my mother was fantastic—that's great, it's wonderful, I love her. So that was how Pearl met my mom and Debbie was such a key part of it. I wish everyone could have been there to see the reaction on my mom's face, on Debbie's face and on Pearl's face.

Pearl, Moe, Bubba, and Debbie

Debbie's 30th Birthday

Debbie turned 30 on August 9, 1989, which was exactly 3 months before she would leave for Israel. Debbie's older sister Brenda had been living in Israel since 1980, was married and eventually would have 2 children. Debbie had never been to Israel until 1988. She had missed her sister's wedding in 1987 due to a Lupus flare-up. In 1988 and 1989 she visited Israel twice with her mother, not only to see her sister Brenda, but also to tour the country. During those two visits, she met two different men. Debbie, I believe, always wanted a permanent relationship, marriage and family. She once said she would give up everything, meaning work, career, etc., if she could find someone who could accept her with her illnesses, lupus and scleroderma. She knew she could not have both, family and career, since it would be too draining and too exhausting for her.

So in 1988 and 1989, during her visits to Israel, even though neither of these men led to a permanent relationship, she came to feel that there would be a better opportunity for her to meet someone in Israel than in the U.S. She also felt that the culture, work environment and overall way of life in Israel would be more suited for her in terms of her illnesses. She would still be able to work full-time and take the afternoons off because of the afternoon break that most Mediterranean countries have. She felt she could then work, lie down and rest and then continue on in the late afternoon and evening hours, which she couldn't do in the United States. Her overall feelings were that moving to Israel would be best for her in terms of coping with her illnesses as well as meeting someone, getting married, having a family and thus, a better life. These are the reasons Debbie eventually moved to Israel in November of 1989.

To return to Debbie's 30th Birthday, the last birthday she celebrated in the U.S. Debbie told both myself and Pearl where she wanted to go, who she wanted to be with and how she wanted to celebrate this, her 30th birthday. Turning 30 was a big event for her, not only because of the number, but she was also leaving the country. She wanted to have the following people share number 30 with her: She wanted me and Pearl, who was soon to become her step-mom. Eileen, her closest friend ever since she was 15. (Eileen eventually got married and had a son named Ian and to this day Eileen is still very close to our family.) When Debbie turned 30 on August 9th, four days later on August 13th would be Eileen's 30th birthday. They were almost like birthday twins, as well as very close personal friends. The other two people were Debbie D. and Jim G.

Both Debbie D and Jim were very active members of the Lupus Foundation of New Jersey, and of its South Jersey Branch; in fact Debbie D was president of the South Jersey Branch of the Lupus Foundation of N.J. Both Jim and Debbie D, were also active on the Board of Directors of the Lupus Foundation of N.J. In 1989, I was president of the Lupus Foundation of N.J. and Pearl was the office manager of the Foundation. There was thus a direct connection between Debbie Liss, Debbie D., Jim, Pearl and myself, and of course that connection was Lupus.

Each year, the Lupus Foundation of America conducted a week-long convention to discuss the latest in treatment, coping mechanisms, as well as providing opportunities for representatives of the various state chapters to meet one another, socialize and share common experiences. Debbie Liss was a representative of the LosAngeles chapter and Jim and Debbie D— were representatives of the N.J. Chapter and that is how they first met one another, at these conventions. As a result of attending these annual conventions (they were party animals), Debbie Liss, Debbie D, and Jim became very close. Thus on August 9, 1989, Debbie Liss selected both of them to attend her 30th birthday in Atlantic City. It was a wonderful day at Atlantic City, I believe everyone even won some money and then, to top the day off, we had dinner at The Meadows at Harrah's Marina Hotel. The Meadows, at that time, was a very, very upscale restaurant I know it cost me a fortune but it was worth every penny and nickel of it. We had a cake, gourmet meal, sang "happy birthday" it was two hours of gracious dining in the middle of our gambling. It was a wonderful, wonderful day. How could any of us have realized that it would be the last time Debbie Liss, Debbie D. and Jim would ever be together. All three passed away in the following seven years.

That is why this story and photo are so very important.

A few months after this photo was taken Debbie Liss left for Israel.

Four years later Debbie D. who had lupus nephritis (kidney involvement) and had been on dialysis for 20 years, passed away. Two years after Debbie D. passed on Jim, who also had serious complications from lupus, passed away. One year after Jim died, Debbie Liss passed away.

The memories of all three being together with Eileen, Pearl and myself on that special day, those memories will last forever—thanks for the beautiful memories.

Jim, Moe, Debbie, Debbie (DiPeppe), Pearl, and Eileen

Debbie and Desert Storm

In November of 1989 Debbie left the United States of America to start her new life in the State of Israel. She settled in the town of Karmiel, where both her mother and her older sister Brenda with her husband Tsion were residing. Her immediate goals were to learn the language, become acclimated, get a job, become an Israeli citizen and find a decent home. Her long range goals were eventually to get married and have a family, which was her main purpose for going to Israel. She felt by 1989 that her quality of life would be much better in Israel and she would also have a better opportunity of meeting someone. Upon arriving in Karmiel, she entered a program called "Ulpan" which is primarily an educational, training and cultural program offered to all new immigrants. This is where she would learn how to read and write Hebrew and eventually lead to making "aliyat" or achieving Israeli citizenship. She had no background in Hebrew, other than the limited amount she learned in Hebrew School, preparing for her Bat Mitzvah. However, before long she was able to communicate in Hebrew and did make "aliyat," Debbie became an Israeli citizen, thus she had dual citizenship, both American and Israeli. She eventually did get a job with a small insurance agency. Since she had a background in America with an insurance company, it was easy for her to transfer those skills into selling insurance, primarily to English speaking Israelis. Thus, within her first year in Israel, Debbie became a citizen, learned the language, obtained a job, found an apartment, made new friends and became integrated into her new society.

It was only a little after the time that Debbie arrived in Israel, January 1991, that America became involved in Desert Storm. Saddam Hussein invaded Kuwait, which the Americans took as an invasion of their sphere of influence in the Middle East and immediately mobilized and eventually sent troops into Kuwait and Saudi Arabia.

Those of us who could remember back to 1991, remember that Desert Storm was a war that was played out on T.V. before our eyes. Every evening, CNN had live footage of the war itself, including missile attacks that the Iraqis launched on Kuwait and Saudi Arabia and eventually on Israel. This is where the story of Debbie and Desert Storm really begins.

Soon enough when Saddam Hussein was being hit by the American Armed Forces, he decided he was going to attack Israel with Scud missiles. Israeli homes had been, for a long time, equipped with one room, what they call an air-tight room, in preparation for any kind of an attack, whether it be by bombs, missiles or even chemical and biological weapons. Israeli homes either had a basement where people could go for shelter or they had, in their individual apartments, a room that was built to specifications to be air-tight. Whenever the air raid alert sounded, the people in Israel would quickly go to their designated area, either a bomb shelter in the basement or an air-tight room in their apartment.

Debbie's apartment had an air-tight room. Also, every man, woman and child in Israel had a gas mask, in case of a chemical or biological attack. Their instructions were, that as soon as the air raid alarm sounded, they should quickly go to their rooms and put on their gas masks. The first time the scuds attacked Israel, Pearl and I were sitting in our living room, watching the war on CNN. The commentator announced there were scuds headed into Israel. The phone rang, and sure enough, there was a collect call from Debbie. She was in her self-contained room and literally crying out for help. "Daddy, they are bombing us and I don't know what to do, this is all new to me, should I put on my mask? If I put on my mask I can't talk to you, if I talk to you I can't put on my mask. What should I do?" Of course Daddy is supposed to have all the answers. Here I am 6000 miles away in my living room, actually watching as these scud missiles are being sent from Iraq to Israel. Fortunately, Saddam didn't have the straightest shooters and most of the scuds missed their targeted areas.

The first response I had was, "Debbie, get the hell out of there and come back home. I know that this is your main goal, to start a new life and improve the quality of your life but, I don't believe your quality of life is being improved sitting in an air-tight room with a gas mask on." Debbie's response was, "I am not leaving, I am an Israeli now even though I am an American citizen. I feel I can make a better life, I just want to survive the next few months, or whatever it is going to take to win this war— and tell President Bush to hurry up and end it quickly."

Well, this scenario played over again every night for the next three or four weeks. It seemed that Iraq just wanted to bomb Israel with those scud missiles. Every night we would receive a collect phone call from Debbie just needing to talk. By this time she had accepted the fact that this was going to be a daily routine and most Israelis' now accepted the fact that they would go on with their lives during the day, continue working or whatever they did and then in the evening wait for the air raid alarm go into their shelters and continue to live that way. And so, every night we received that collect phone call from Debbie. Toward the second or third week she even started laughing about it. She decided to bring her T.V. set into her air-tight room and just relax and hope that this guy Saddam Hussein would keep on missing his targets. We just continued to talk with her for as long as the alarm was on and until the all clear signal and then she would say, "Good night, I love you." and that was the end of the call.

I have to say "thank God" that Desert Storm ended pretty quickly, because when we received that month's telephone bill, there was over $1000.00 in collect calls from Israel. I said if this war lasts very long I am going to be bankrupt. There is no way I can afford $1000 in phone bills every month. There is no way I can tell my daughter to stop calling because I know that these calls, and the reassurance that we could give her, were essential for her survival.

And so day after day we would wait for her calls and continue the dialogue until finally the missiles stopped, the war came to an end and the phone company lost a major account.

The Birth of Debbie's Niece, Ronit

In 1991, Debbie's second year in Israel, her sister Brenda became pregnant for the first time and as the months went by we anxiously awaited the birth of our first grandchild, and Debbie the birth of her first niece.

In August 1991, Pearl and I flew to Israel to be with Brenda, her husband Tsion and Debbie at this blessed event. I have said that birthdays were very special for my children and especially for Debbie. Every one of her birthdays was a very special occasion and she made sure of that.

As August rolled around it was getting closer to Debbie's birthday, and she became very concerned that Brenda's baby might be born on *her* special day. She didn't want to share her birthday with anyone and—Brenda was still holding on.

It was August 8 and still no sign of any movement and of course the following day would be August 9, Debbie's birthday. Finally, it is August 9th, 1991 and we are about to celebrate Debbie's 32nd birthday.

In the center of Karmiel, the city in Israel where both Brenda and Debbie lived, there is a shopping center. It includes various stores and shops, eateries and an ice cream parlor, that Pearl and I liked to go to whenever we were visiting Israel. We had decided that we would celebrate Debbie's birthday at this special ice cream parlor.

So here were Debbie, Brenda, Tsion, Pearl and myself, on August 9th, celebrating Debbie's birthday, when Brenda says, " I am getting contractions," There is no hospital in Karmiel, the nearest is in Zefat, about 25 miles north, and that of course was where Brenda would have to go to deliver her baby.

Debbie begins saying to her sister, "you better not give birth today! Not only don't I want to share my birthday with my niece/nephew, I want it to be very special for her/him as well. So Brenda, you better hold on for another day or so." But the pains were coming more frequently and

Brenda and Tsion soon decided to go to the hospital. Now Debbie, Pearl and I were left at the ice cream parlor and Debbie kept repeating, "My sister better not have that baby today, she better not give birth to that baby today. I don't want two people in the family to share the same birthday."

Well, thank God, Brenda did not give birth to that baby on the 9th; it was false labor. Brenda came back to Karmiel later that night, and two days later on August 11, 1991, our first granddaughter and Debbie's first niece, a very healthy baby girl, Ronit Fern Bitan was born. Of course Debbie said, "Thank you, Brenda for not having Ronit on my birthday."

Introduction to Debbie and Gershon

When Debbie arrived in Israel in 1989, as I mentioned in another part of this book, she had a number of major goals. To make aliyat—become a citizen of Israel, learn the language, become a part of Israeli life, which included getting a job, home and hopefully marrying. By 1991 Debbie was successful in many of her goals. She had made aliyat, she completed ulpan (an intensive 6 month program to learn to speak, read and write the language), she obtained a job selling insurance and she was also able to complete examinations in Hebrew so that she could get her insurance certification. She was very successful in her business aspect. She also was able to purchase a home during her years in Israel. But one of her major goals (I am not placing them in any particular order), was the very important goal of developing a lasting relationship, one she hoped would lead to marriage and family.

It was just about this time that she met Gershon. Gershon was divorced with three daughters, working in the shipyards of Haifa. They met, and immediately it looked like there was some chemistry between them, and they began a relationship. The relationship included them spending time away. They went to Eilat, a major resort in Israel, for a long weekend. I remember Debbie sending us photographs of the two of them in Eilat. Gershon introduced Debbie to his daughters and his mom and it seemed like it was headed in the right direction as far as Debbie was concerned. Eventually, Debbie began to push Gershon a little in terms of what he was looking for in this relationship—did he see any possibility of it becoming a lasting and permanent relationship, marriage and family? Or, was it just going to be an intimate relationship without any commitment? About a year into the relationship, when Debbie began to push for some commitment from Gershon, he basically made it clear to Debbie that although he cares about her, she is a wonderful, beautiful person and he does not think, at this point in his life, he is interested in making any commitment to marriage and family. If Debbie feels that's the only thing she wants from the relationship, than they should not continue. Gershon, I believe, made it very clear to Debbie at that point that he was not interested in marriage. In all the conversations that we had with Debbie over the next five years—the relationship continued actually until Debbie's passing—Debbie kept expressing the hope that Gershon would change. Pearl and I, spent many, many days with Gershon and Debbie when we visited Israel. Debbie made sure we would spend time with them both, so we got to know him fairly well and there was no question in our minds that he was not going to make any commitment. I will never understand what it is with women, whether it is my daughter or any woman, why they feel they can change their men.

It seems like that is one of their purposes in life—to change men. When Debbie bought a new home, she made sure it had an extra bedroom, so that at anytime his youngest daughter could stay with them. Debbie told me, "don't worry Daddy, I am going to change him, he is going to eventually marry me, we are eventually going to live together first and then marry." She was so sure that this relationship was at least going to be a "living together relationship," which in fact never happened.

Gershon was never really committed to the ongoing relationship. There were many times when Debbie would be waiting on a Friday night for him to come spend Shabbat with her, after visiting his children in Tiberias. She was continuously disappointed during that period of time. It was painful for Pearl and me, because we knew how much Debbie cared about him, loved him and how much she wanted Gershon to be the person she would share her life with. Unfortunately, Gershon was not the man till the day she passed away; he was never the man for her. The tragedy of this relationship is that there were many times that Debbie would be waiting for him, preparing a meal for him, waiting to see him and he would not show. He gave one reason after another—if not his mother, his children, or his work would keep him away.

In Judaism there is a mourning period called "shiva," where friends and family sit for 7 days. After Debbie passed away Gershon came every day and every night. He was there for Debbie after she passed away but he had never been there for Debbie when she really needed him—to share a life with her.

Pearl's Stories

Toilet Paper Story

When Debbie knew we were planning a trip to Israel in 1990, my first time over, she said, "Pearl, you must bring your own toilet paper with you, I carry a roll in my purse at all times." I laughed but she said, "It is the truth, because the toilet paper in Israel is hard and stiff." She insisted I must bring rolls of toilet paper with me. So I listened and I did pack a few rolls in my suitcase.

Debbie picked us up at the airport that beautiful October evening, and it really was a beautiful evening .

It was also my daughter Jaime's first trip, not only to Israel, but outside the United States. After going through customs, Debbie and I headed for the bathroom, my first experience in an Israeli public rest room. There we were, Debbie and I handing back and forth, underneath the stall, American toilet paper. We both giggled and laughed the whole time. We were back and forth underneath the stall like a Seinfeld episode—underneath, underneath, underneath.

Afterthought: That October evening, I mentioned was beautiful. I never saw a moon like the moon that I saw that night in Israel. And to this day, I have never seen a moon so big and beautiful as the one I saw in Israel my very first visit. I felt as if it was ordered special—just for me.

The Lawrence Taylor (LT) Story

Debbie was a big New York Giants football fan. In fact, our entire family are big fans of the Giants. As you know, Debbie had lupus, an autoimmune disease. From the time Debbie was diagnosed with lupus, both Moe and I had been active members of the Lupus Foundation of New Jersey.

The foundation held various fund raising events each year for research and public awareness and we both took an active role in this area. One of their events, the annual fashion show, was held every October and their goal was to always recruit some celebrities from the New York/New Jersey area to participate. It was the year 1992 that the New York Giants became part of our fashion show. This involvement became possible due to the efforts of Karl Nelson, a lineman of the Giants, who earlier that year graciously accepted the post of spokesperson for the Lupus Foundation of New Jersey.

The evening of the big event many of the Giants attended and escorted our models down the runway, and in fact many of the models were the wives of the New York Giants. Lawrence Taylor (LT) one of the all-time great professional player, attended. He was gracious, mingling with our crowd and many of us wanted photographs with him. Debbie, who was visiting us from Israel, was one of the attendees who couldn't wait to stand next to him and have her photograph taken. It was a thrill for Debbie as she stood proudly next to this 6'4" giant of a man. Debbie was petite in size, her height 4'11", which really made them look like an 'odd couple'.

Well, the photograph came out beautifully and I added to our family gallery—Debbie standing next to Lawrence Taylor. (See photograph on next page.)

It was the winter of 1992, and my mother-in-law Esther, Moe's mother and Debbie's Bubba, was visiting us. She began to glance at all the photographs hanging on the wall, the wall that we lovingly refer to as 'our family gallery'. Esther always enjoyed seeing photos of her family. When she came upon Debbie's photograph with Lawrence Taylor, she took a long hard look. Finally, in her very sweet Yiddish voice and grandmotherly way she asked "Debbie goes with him? He's so tall." I smiled and said, "Oh no, he is just a good friend."

I laughed to myself, shared the story with Debbie and Moe and we all had a good belly laugh over the comments. It is a Debbie story I will never forget. Each time I re-tell the story it brings both tears of laughter and tears of missing Debbie to my eyes.

Debbie and Lawrence Taylor

Kayaking on the Jordan River

In the summer of 1993, Moe, Jaime and I visited Debbie in Israel. Debbie was dating Gershon and she was anxious for us to meet him. Gershon had 3 daughters from a previous marriage. Debbie and Gershon planned a fun day for us, we were to go kayaking on the Jordan River and afterward have a barbecue on the banks of the Jordan. It sounded so wonderful, kayaking on the Jordan River in Israel followed by a picnic on the banks of the Jordan—what could be better? Gershon and his youngest daughter, Edit, arrived at Debbie's and we all piled into the car for our new experience. When we got to the Jordan there was a line to rent the kayaks. Gershon got on line and rented three kayaks. There were 2 people to a kayak, and we paired off: Moe and I, Debbie and Jaime and Gershon and Edit. We headed down the Jordan. We all had a memorable kayaking experience, one that I will never forget.

Well, now it is time to picnic. Debbie packed a great lunch and Gershon was in charge of making the fire for the barbecue. We had all worked up an appetite ... we were starving. Gershon prepares to make the fire, no, he is not opening a bag of charcoal briquettes and a can of starter, he is gathering up twigs and sticks and adding these little pieces of charcoal that he carried with him from home. You read it correct: twigs and sticks." Moe and I looked at each other and we both thought ... well, that's how they make their cookouts in Israel. Well, Gershon begins his dance with the twigs, sticks, coals and plain old matches, and what a dance it was. As soon as a little fire begins to flicker that is exactly how fast the flicker went out. Time is passing and we are all looking at each other. I am telling Moe, Debbie and Jaime under my breath that we are all very hungry and the leaves on the trees are starting to look tasty, let's forget about barbecuing and just eat the other food Debbie prepared. Everyone is afraid to hurt Gershon's feelings and Gershon continues to work and work at starting a fire but with absolutely no luck. Fortunately for us, another family that was cooking out offered us their hot coals to cook with, They took pity on us, probably observing the hungry looks on our faces and seeing Gershon making a fool of himself.

After we had eaten and sat around talking, we Americans agreed that Israel needs to import barbecue briquettes. They would make a fortune because most Israelis use the twig method for making outdoor barbecues.

We laughed at our cookout adventure for days even Gershon laughed. By the way, we still think we can make a fortune selling briquettes to the Israelis.

Daddy's 60th Surprise Birthday

It was February, 1993 and Debbie was in the States visiting with us. I told Debbie I was planning a 60th Birthday for Moe, her Daddy, in September. It was going to be a surprise. Since we both knew she was not going to be able to fly back to the states in September, and that Moe and I would be going to Israel in August, we knew we could plan a special surprise for his birthday in September. We put our heads together and decided that I would make a video of Debbie delivering a special birthday message to her Daddy when we were in Israel that August Debbie's visit was wonderful but it flew by as it usually did and before we knew it, we were hugging and saying good-bye at the airport.

We talked every week and the topic always came back to the surprise party. We had come up with a great idea …. Debbie could play the guitar, sing and deliver a birthday message on the video. Debbie wanted sheet music for the guitar … she had certain music in mind … my job was to find it in the States and send it over. I did my secret mission, I found the sheet music and sent it off. Debbie was to practice, practice, practice and get herself ready for the big day that I would make her a music video star for her biggest fan, her Daddy.

Well, August came and we arrived in Israel. Debbie and I cooked up a scheme to get Moe out of the house without us. We sent him to Brenda's and told him we would meet him there and that Debbie and I would be doing some shopping in town.

Moe left the house and we got started. Debbie broke out the music and guitar and I readied the video camera. Well, it took quite a few times before we got it right … we giggled and laughed and had re-take and re-take. It was either Debbie cracking up or myself cracking up. Finally the video was completed and we felt it was going to be the best present she could give her Daddy. I packed it away only to be shown on that very special 60th Birthday.

Debbie also wanted to give him a wristwatch so off we went shopping. (Our little lie to get him out of the house really wasn't a lie—we were going shopping) We walked into town and talked about all kinds of things some serious and some not so serious. Debbie and I talked a lot about relationships. How to keep them going and make them strong.

Well, Debbie found the perfect wristwatch and asked me to have it engraved when I got back to the States. I did have the watch engraved with Debbie's words and felt quite honored that Debbie entrusted me with this special gift for her Daddy.

Needless to say, Moe's 60th Birthday was a surprise and Debbie's video the most meaningful gift a Dad could receive from his daughter. The wristwatch, another surprise, one that he will treasure always. Debbie did good for her Daddy's 60th. As for me, I had a great time with Debbie creating the video for her Daddy and my loving husband.

Debbie, Pearl, Dad in AC

In the summer of 1994, Debbie visited us again. It was always fun having Debbie visit. We would shop for all kinds of gifts and special finds for her new found friends in Israel. We would also do a lot of the fun things Debbie loved to do before she made the big move to Israel.

This visit, we decided to take one day and go down to Atlantic City. Debbie loved Atlantic City and loved to gamble, in moderation of course. Black jack and craps were her favorites. So off we went, Debbie, Daddy and me. Daddy, being the great and generous guy that he is, would always give us both money to gamble with, so whether we won or lost we were always winners, and if we actually won at the tables or slots, we would be double winners.

Our ride down was fun talking and sharing all kinds of stories. Once we got to Atlantic City, we all sort of went our separate ways though not too far from one another. Debbie shooting craps, Moe playing blackjack and me enjoying roulette. We would touch base with one another and sometimes cheered each other on. We were having a great time but we were not cleaning up, so to speak, just breaking even. Debbie and I were still winners, as I said, it was gift money we were gambling with.

Just before we were getting ready to leave, Debbie said, let's try the slots. We all sat down at different machines. I, being very cautious and known to be a little hesitant when it comes to gambling, was putting the coins in one at a time, so my coins were lasting a long time. First Moe came over to me, since his coins were long gone, and I continued to put the coins in one at a time. Now Debbie comes over, since she also had depleted all her coins, and there I am still putting my coins in one at a time. Debbie said, "Pearl, what are you doing? Come on, put more than one coin in at a time, we will be here all night at the rate you are going." I started to put 3 and 4 coins at the same time and lo and behold I hit a great big jack pot … the coins came pouring out as we all stood there wide eyed. My jackpot was $250.00—not too shabby. Debbie and I ordered drinks to celebrate. She had a Baileys and I had a coffee. We laughed out loud, Debbie and I saying, "Boy, was I a big, big winner—a jack pot plus free money to start with." We walked out of the casino still drinking—Debbie her Baileys, and me with my coffee. To this day, I still have the glass and the purple cup we drank from. I still drink my coffee in the purple cup, and every time I do, I think of Debbie and our AC adventure.

Josie's (Pearl's Mom) Story

I knew Debbie a short time but I felt like I knew her forever. Every time we got together at her Dad's and Pearl's home, we would talk and have a lot of fun. Debbie would sit there look at me and say, "Josie, you feel like having a Brandy Alexander?" Then I would say "Debbie I would love one." So we would both drink a Brandy Alexander. Then she would say, "maybe we should have another," and I would say, "Oh, no, my daughter won't want me to have another."

Debbie wrote me wonderful letters and I would read them over and over again. I still hold those letters dear to me, and still read them again and again.

Debbie was the dearest, she was wonderful and I loved her very much and will never forget her as long as I live.

Debbie told me one time that she went on a vacation to Turkey. She mentioned to me that many Israelis go to Turkey to gamble and Debbie loved to gamble. So while the whole family was sitting in my daughter's living room, she said to her Uncle Murray, "I won a million lire." I said, "Debbie you're a millionaire!" and Debbie said, "$400.00 in American money." That was Debbie.

Another "Bubba" Story

Debbie left the States for her new home in Israel in November 1989. During the period 1989 to the time she passed away, August, 1996, she would come and visit once or twice a year to see Pearl and me, our family, her mother's family, friends, etc. Her mother had also moved to Israel in 1989, but had all her family here, so when Debbie came to the States it was to see both sides of her family—her father, Pearl, Jaime, her uncle and aunt, and also to see her bubba and her mother's family who lived close by as well. She would come in for 2 to 3 weeks at a time and travel around New York and New Jersey and sometimes even to Louisville, Kentucky, or Detroit, where some of her mother's family lived.

The incident that I am going to relate here concerns my mother, who at this time is in her early nineties. My mother is at our house to spend some time with Debbie and have dinner with us. Mom was living at the Daughters of Miriam Home in Clifton, which was very close by. When Debbie came to visit us, of course, we wanted to make sure that she spent as much time with her Bubba as possible. It was a Saturday afternoon, and though my mother would usually take a nap in the afternoon, this Saturday she wanted to spend time with her granddaughter, "Debbila" as she fondly referred to Debbie. Whenever Debbie came to the states, she always wanted to see some of the latest movies. We had rented a movie called "Fatal Attraction" with Sharon Stone and Michael Douglas, which was the "hot flick" of that year. It was a "steamy" movie that Debbie really wanted to see She felt that it would be a good movie to watch in the afternoon, because her Bubba would probably be sleeping. Debbie and Bubba were in the living room and Debbie said to her Bubba, "I'm going to watch a movie that I would like to see and you can sleep." Bubba said, "so what is the name of the movie ?"

"Fatal Attraction", says Debbie, "but really, it is not one that you would like."

Debbie puts on the movie, and you remember that the very opening scene is about as steamy and raw as any scene can be. Now here is my mother and her granddaughter watching this opening scene and all of a sudden my mother yells out in Yiddish, *"Kourva"* which translated literally means "slut" or "tramp". She is saying this to Debbie while putting her hands over Debbie's eyes. "Don't watch this movie—she is no good, she is a *Kourva*." Well, you had to see this to believe it. Here is a ninety something grandmother trying to protect her thirty something granddaughter from seeing this movie. Now what is even more amazing, that after this particular scene and after she did this to Debbie, and as the movie continues for another 2 hours never once did my mother, Debbie's grandmother, ever shut her eyes. This is the first time she ever went without an afternoon nap. She just sat for 2 hours, glued to the TV, watching this movie that she had tried to protect her granddaughter from seeing. It was a sight to behold. Pearl and I had already seen the movie but we saw a greater movie seeing grandmother and granddaughter sitting on the coach, arms around each other, watching "Fatal Attraction."

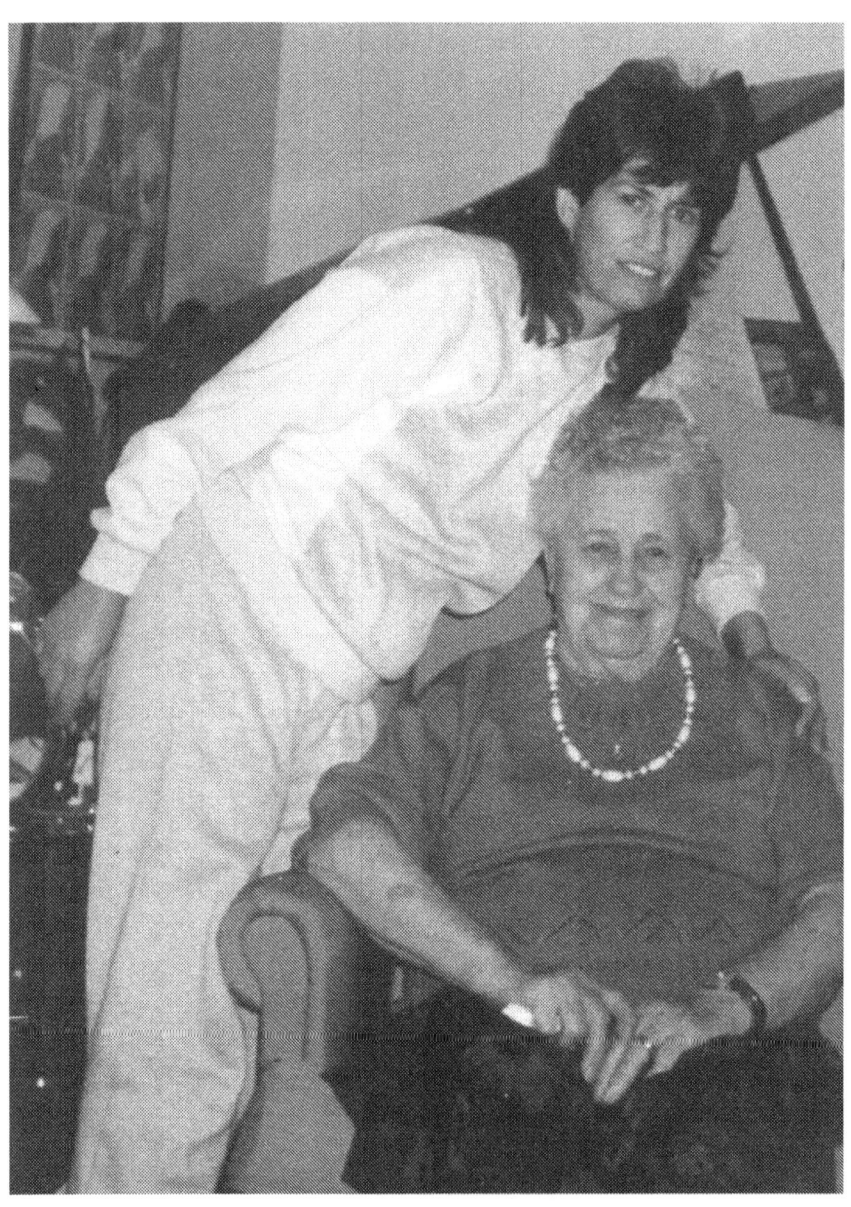

Debbie and Bubba

Jeff Liss' Stories

I remember going to Chinese restaurants when we were young. Debbie didn't like Chinese food, so she would order a cream cheese and jelly sandwich. First of all, have you ever heard of a Chinese restaurant that served cream cheese and jelly? She wouldn't eat the Chinese food but, I believe, she would eat the soup. How taste buds and times change. Later in her life, Chinese food was one of her favorite foods.

To be a New York sports fan is to know that you go through every new season with renewed hope of a Championship. My sister loved sports and carried the torch, even when she moved to California. Debbie was an especially devoted Mets fan. Whenever they would make their west coast swing, we would, many times, go to San Francisco and San Diego to watch them play. To all the sports teams and the players that we agonized with, laughed at, yelled, cried and enjoyed special moments with thank you, for making my sister and me just a little bit closer, especially the...

N.Y. Mets, 1969 and 1986 World Champions
New York Knicks, 1969 and 1973 World Champions
New York Rangers, 1994 Stanley Cup Champions
New York Giants, 1986 and 1990 World Champions

Debbie had waited years for one of her stocks to hit it "big". When it finally hit, she asked me, "When should I sell it." I told her, "when you feel you have made the money that you wanted." She told me, in a sad but serious voice, "I've waited this long for this stock to make money and I now would trade it all just to be healthy." Debbie never was able to use that money she made, but that money helped pay for my wedding.

When I was in Israel, in the summer of 1996, just before her passing, I was talking to Debbie about reincarnation and what her beliefs were on the subject. I told her that I had watched a very informative movie about the subject called, "The Little Budda" and maybe a video store in Israel would have it. She had never heard of the movie. A few hour later, she was looking through the T.V. Guide in the newspaper and she said, "Is this the movie you were talking about…it is on Israeli T.V. tonight." Together, we watched the movie that night.

Just before Debbie passed on, she put air conditioning into her condo. She knew she wasn't going to be around to use it. She put it in so that it would be more comfortable for my mother, who would inherit the condo after Debbie's passing.

The Meaning of My Life

When Debbie was diagnosed, in April 1996, with fourth stage lung cancer, which had already metastasized to her bones, she knew that her days on this earth were very short. She began to take a look at her life and felt somewhat disappointed that she had not left her "mark on this world." Debbie never married, never had children, and therefore felt she was leaving nothing of herself behind.

She there upon sent letters to all her family, friends and associates in which she asked them, "How Have I Touched Your Life?" It was important for her to know, "Was my life meaningful to you?"

Following are excerpts from the responses she received. I will indicate who the person was, as to the relationship to Debbie, following each letter:

(Unfortunately, the following letter was written, after Debbie's death).

"Thanks Debbie!

"The Debbie I knew was a very brave woman. During the period of our close friendship (1987-89), she was in the midst of a prolonged battle with physical illness, Lupus. I remember it was especially a downer for Debbie to be living within 3 blocks of the ocean, yet rarely experience the sand and surf due to the risk of sun exposure.

To me Debbie was a pilgrim. She was the first person from my home town to move to California and my first friend to make the transition back to the soul level. It was through Debbie's connections that I secured a rent-controlled apartment in Santa Monica. While there, I halted a ten year battle with alcoholism. Yes, I still carry many warm feelings for Debbie in my heart. The most important thing Debbie ever gave me was encouragement. You see, I am a stand-up comedian and Debbie was for a long time the only friend to show interest in my talent Even the last time we spoke, her last week on this planet, she once again inquired about how my comedy career was developing. Virtually no one else had ever validated my dreams. Debbie was different in this way and for her loving encouragement, I have undying gratitude.

Well, my words are obviously too late for Debbie to read personally, but I believe her family is still assembling the collection. With that in mind, this letter stands as my Thank You card to Debbie Liss. Her life was significant and will never be forgotten"

Love and Blessings
Dan O'Connor (Debbie's brother's close friend)

P.S. This letter was the first piece written by a set of Hebrew pencils. Debbie willed these pencils to me so I may write my comedy!

Dear Debby

"Sheesh girl, this sounds like a high school English composition assignment! *How Debby Liss has Touched My Life, 200-400 words, due Thursday.* (I wonder if I'll be marked off for misspelled words…)

I guess when I think of you, I think of strength, competence and humor, all characteristics which I very much value. You are one of the few single women I know (besides myself) who made "aliyat" and just knowing that there is someone out there who has dealt with the same problems has been a great savior to my sanity at times.

I have an enormous amount of respect and admiration for your success in gaining sufficient competence in Hebrew to pass your boards here and work in the competitive and, let's face it, sexist world of insurance. You manage to provide your clients with a level of service hard to find in Israel. And invested a lot of time and energy in the synagogue. And all this while dealing with ongoing medical problems which would reduce that average person to a pathetic, sniveling jellyfish. Somehow, your forthright sense of humor and strength of character allow you to function at a higher level than most of the "normal" population.

That's it toots! You're such a terrific person that I even forgive you for rejecting Rudy's advances, though Rudy still lives in hope that you will one day be converted to a cat fancier and will spend hours cuddling and patting him"

Leah (friend living in Karmiel, Israel)

Debbie

"Our friendship has grown out of working together on the Board of the Congregation and in handling my family's insurance needs. I have always been impressed by your integrity, dedication vision, hard work and incredible inner strength. It took me a year to finally decide about the policy for me, but you stuck with me, answered questions, explained and *never* pushed. I value greatly the extra time you made to have a cup of coffee, talk and get to know each other.

I trust you, Debbie. I would like to think that our friendship helps to support you now. I promise to work together with you to do so."

"A faithful friend is the medicine of life"…..Ben Sira 6, 18

Lori (friend)

Dear Debbie

"After our talk the other night, I had a dream. I hope I can share it in a way you can understand. It was incredibly beautiful and powerful.

The dream started out about me visiting you. Since my spiritual teacher is also in New York, I thought about going and visiting her at the same time and taking you with me to meet her. In the dream, we went up to meet her. I whispered to one of the aides that I wanted to introduce you and that you had cancer. When we went up to Gurumayi, we kneeled and bowed, you became in the middle of a mother of pearl shell. The light was illuminating all around you. The quote, "it is the sand that causes irritation to form the pearl" As I looked at you, you were like this huge luminescent pearl within the mother of pearl shell. There was incredible white and golden light everywhere. In the dream, I just stayed with the white and gold light. Part of me said, I should write it down then, but I know by the intensity of the experience, I would remember everything and I just couldn't tear myself away from the incredible light.

I somehow felt that the dream itself was a gift for both of us and healing".

"Today is your birthday."

Love,
Diane (Debbie's former therapist in California)

Dear Debbie

"Thank you for your note inviting me to share how you have touched my life…

No one but the two of us know about our conversations about the Mikes, the Rays, the Gershons of this world. If there's one thing we have in common, it's the "broken heart syndrome".

You, with your elegant professional veneer, and I with my abrasive surface, surely appear to most of the people we have known as being fully in control of our love-lives. You and I both know nothing could be further from the truth!

Regardless of the differences in our ages, our backgrounds, our professions, we remain "sisters-under-the-skin", when it comes to this area of our private worlds. The times we giggled, cursed, nodded knowingly, got a little maudlin…This is something I have shared with no one else in Israel, the way I have with you…

Thank you for letting me be a part of your life. You have certainly enriched mine…"

Much love,
Sylvia (friend)

Dear Debbie

As I think back over the 4+ years I've lived in Karmiel, I remember the many, many times that your voice on the phone, or you reassuring me as we chatted in my home, gave me *peace of mind.* I know that you would be there for me if and when I needed your help and assistance. Never have I had an insurance agent like you!! You are the best in what you do. I praise you and your business know-how to all. But truly, I feel this "giving" and "caring" in business is only a reflection of you—of your personality—the true Debbie.

It has been, and continues to be, a delight to know you. You are an important part of my life here in Israel.

As I know you would be with me in my time of need—I want to be with you—whenever and however you need me—just call—I'm here for you.

My love and prayers are with you."

Barbara (friend)

Dear Debbie

"Hey! How are you doing? What's going on? I just wanted to say hi. I graduate Friday…it's finally here…free at last. Well, anyway, I hear you're coming here in November, very cool. I can't wait to see you. I like your new hair, it looks good on you. Anyway, I just wanted to say my thoughts and my love are with you and if you ever need to vent or just talk or complain, I have two really good ears. Anytime, it doesn't matter when. Well, I'll talk to you soon."

Love always,
Jaime (Debbie's step-sister)

Dear Debbie

"As I start this letter, my mind goes back to 1979, when we first met, 17 years! We had just bought the building when Santa Monica's dwellers and landlords declared a Civil War.

You were neutral and I welcome your attitude with all my heart, and deep into it, I placed you as a friend.

You are still there, and I'm still grateful.

I'm very sorry and concerned about your health, but I'm also convinced that you are in the best place and the best hands to nurse you back to a full recovery. We are praying for you.

May the sun shine on your health, your life and your adored country".

With love
Ricardo (former landlord in Santa Monica and friend)

Debbie

"Laughter in the face of adversity can really help a lot. Trying to keep a positive outlook is probably difficult, but is assuredly one of the most beneficial "treatments" you can give yourself. I know that you are no stranger to tough challenges. That is why I feel you have what it takes to meet this one head on—and conquer it! The fears will be pushed aside with your positive, peaceful inner spirit.

My prayers and thoughts are with you. I'll write again soon."

Peace and Love,
Chuck Lambert (friend of your Dad)
….let me add, and cancer survivor.

Hi Deb,

"Do you remember the first time we met? It was late one Saturday night, after Jeff and I had been "out on the booze". You came out to give us a hard time for being drunk and "farting" all over your living room and for Jeff for feeding his guest those frozen burritos.

So how didn't you touch my life. If it hadn't been for you, I wouldn't have met Jeff, stayed in L.A., met the wife, had the kids, got the mortgage and still be working a 60-8- week…well they are cute kids.

Then there were all the other "Kiwis" too, remember Craig, Beaver and Kent?

My wife was also telling me that on the first Valentines together. I gave you and her the same red rose—so you know that went over real big.

I thought we had some pretty good times, hanging out, mostly just good clean fun.

So, while you haven't walked on the moon or carved a Michelangelo, your life is of no less important than those people. You were an emotional springboard/safety net to so many…me, Jeff, all the Kiwis.

I just remembered something else. The first time I got my hair permed, walked into the apartment, here were you, Jeff, Tom. You and Maureen were the only ones to say it looked good, the others were only giving me a hard time.

So this isn't goodbye…it's till we meet again."
John (close friend of brother Jeff)

Debbie

"Hopefully, you're sleeping (after a lousy week of doctors, disappointment and dilemma) with wonderful dreams of flowers, sunlight, peace and happiness, with a couple of really great looking studs thrown in for good luck!

I've been trying for a couple of weeks to write about this girl, Debbie Liss and who she is for me. It's hard to sum up a person in a couple of sheets of notepaper, but okay.

Debbie has lupus and scleroderma and cancer. Debbie's the girl who had long, lovely tresses and now has fuzz on top. But that's not who Debbie is to me.
You're smart as a whip and cool as a mint julep in August. You have a knife-edge sharp sense of humor that only comes out of New York and New Jersey.

You're my expert on sports; my super-expert on insurance. No one I've ever met devotes so much time and thought to her clients!

You're this tiny (compared to me!) BIG person that I can't squeeze anymore and that's a real pity for me, but you're probably lucky cause I hug too hard sometimes.

Debbie's this kid, but not really. Often you are this mature woman with thought and emotions beyond your years and then…whoops!…you're a crazy nut with whacky notions that make me laugh.

Somehow, you and the men in your life are the first thing I remember about you…the guy in Tiberias—wrong! The guy in Karmiel—wrong! Gershon - right and wrong, right and wrong, etc. etc. My heart went out to you with some of these affairs

You love so many people but I doubt whether you know how many people really love you. You've touched more lives than you can even imagine.

Debbie, you're my friend, but you're much more than that. You're my American pal, my buddy in Israel, even my soulmate at times, and…my child. Maybe that's the thing, Debbie, I love you as I love my own children."

Always and forever,
Leona (close friend)

Dear Debbie

"Well I wrote pretty much everything on the letter. I am sorry I will not be coming with my mom. I would have like to seen you. I hope you like this card. I am sorry I couldn't have given you the smile personally. I can't really relate to the pain you are going through but I can understand. And I wish there was a way I can take away some of that pain. I promise you I will keep sending you cards and letters to keep you a little busy reading. Maybe it will help you be a little stronger and put a smile on your face. It is real important to keep strong, it always makes things easier.

Anyways, I hope you enjoy the letter and card and you will get another one soon. How are those books mom sent you? I didn't know you were so interested in baseball. My mom bought 10 sport books. I will write again."

Fraydle (young cousin of Debbie's)

Debbie

"Hi! It seems like only yesterday since I last saw you. The years fly by faster and faster every year. I can hardly believe I'm going to be 40 years old this year! A lot has happened over these past ten years or so. I'm sure my mom has kept you up to date, as she has for me about you.

I think of you often. I worry every time I hear about a bombing in Israel. I don't know exactly where you live and travel to, I can only pray that you're safe and doing well.

I don't listen to very much music these days. However, when I do listen to music, or play my guitar, it's usually 70's. Songs that remind me of times when life was simple (although it seemed very complicated at the time). So much of that music reminds me of the good times we shared together

I still play the song I wrote for you. One day I'll make a recording and send it to you.

It breaks my heart to hear how sick you've been. I only wish you were closer so I could see you or at least talk to you. I heard you might be coming back to the States. Please let me know when so we can get together. I would really like to see you. If you feel up to writing, you can write me at my business address. I'll write again soon, and send some pictures. Please take care of yourself and send my best to your mom and sister. I might try and see your dad if he still lives in the same place. Take care, I love you!"

Always
Dave (Debbie's first real boyfriend,
they remained in touch with each other for 20 years)

Debbie

"I want you to know that even though we are thousands of miles apart, my thoughts are on you a great deal. I think back to the times when you were a little girl and I was a teenager. No one could have imagined where life would take us, or where it will take us forward. I believe that some day we will connect with all our friends and family in a better place, a place where everyone is vibrant and healthy. It is this thought that helps me deal with the pain and tragedies of everyday life. I hope that there are some thoughts that will help you find peace in the agony you are in.

I am praying for a miracle for you. If you need anything, I am here for you."

Love
Barry (Debbie's cousin)

Dear Debbie

Things with us are pretty much the same and, as always, we are thinking of you. The last few times we called, you were resting, and we did not want to disturb you.

We often talk about our visit to Israel and especially the time we spent with you. We can't forget that you went out and bought special food that you knew we liked. I can still taste that delicious "yogurt" that is really sour cream. We will never forget your kindness to us.

We also talk about the time you spent with us before you moved to Israel. We do not have a daughter and somehow you took the place of one. It was a great experience for us, and the house became very empty after you left.

We especially remember the times you were with Bubba. She so enjoyed every time you pronounced BUBBA!!! She was so glad and happy when you were with her. She always had a soft spot for "Debbie the smart one." She is very proud that her granddaughter could go out in the business world and sell insurance.

We knew that you are a fighter (you have always been one) and you will beat this illness. You have always made your own way, and you are one of the most independent and courageous persons we know.

Debbie, we always think of you, we always have. We want you to know we love you very much!"

Your loving Aunt and Uncle
Rose and Murray

Dear Debbie,

"Thanks for helping me make my trip to Israel a more spiritual and enlightened time. Spending these days with you and counseling with you on a different level, has been very beautiful for me.

I am very proud of you. You are fighting adversity and being very strong. As your soul and spirit grow everyday, like all of us, it will be much easier for you.

You helped make your home mine for two weeks and I enjoyed that. I will work on keeping that last egg consciousness throughout my days. When we believe it won't crack, it won't."

Love
Jeff (Debbie's brother)

Dear Debbie

"Hi! I decided I would write on my word processor. Maybe I won't make so many spelling errors. I'm sending you the two tapes, I really liked the "Cutting Edge." I've watched it a few times when it came on TV. You said you thought you saw it. It has some great ice skating in it and I thought it was funny so you might want to see it again. I'm not sure about the Whoopi Goldberg movie. She is coming out with a new movie called "Eddie," where she is the coach of the New York Knicks.

I just wanted to take this opportunity to tell you something. I'm not sure if you realized that as far as I'm concerned, you witnessed a miracle.

When you told me the story about our parents hugging together with you and Mother doing Daddy's laundry and them eating together…to me, that is a miracle. I don't know anything in my lifetime that is bigger or more miraculous that that. Yes, I'm including the Mets in '69. This will have a positive effect on all of us in our family. I am so glad that Ronit and Shai will be around more positive energy when our parents are together. It takes much pressure off me to always wonder how my parents are going to act when they are together. You have made it possible! I thank you with all my heart for being the vehicle to bring them to a higher level.

I realize it must be weird talking to me about certain things. I'm no longer that partying drunk just out for a good time. It's hard for people that know me to accept that I have changed and that I can have deep soul conversations. I've been studying different concepts about life from different avenues to figure out what makes sense for my life.

That doesn't mean it will work for you or anybody else. I've done more spiritual growth in the last 2 years than my first 32. There is countless knowledge in the universe for me to grasp. This is never ending. I realize you are going through a hard time right now. I am open to help you in whichever avenue you choose. It is your choice. Take care."

Love
Jeff (Debbie's brother)

Dear Debbie

"I am writing this letter to tell you how important you are to me now, have been and will always be. First, I want to express to you my feelings about who you are and some of the important moments of your life and how they also relate to us.

I want you to know, if you haven't figured it out yet, that you are the "apple of my eye." I have always had the greatest amount of love for you in every aspect of your life, from early childhood, through your hectic teenage years and as an adult.

As I sit here writing this letter, I'm reliving some of those unforgettable moments do you remember them?

Remember the time you gave a report on the opera, "The Marriage of Figaro" in the 2nd or 3rd grade? I took time off from work to sit in the back of your classroom at School #26 in Paterson. Was your teacher Ms. Oliver? I'll never forget how you described the "interaction" between Figaro, Suzannah, the Count and Countess.

Or the time I came home from working in the Philadelphia Prison System and there, sitting in our living room, were you and Eileen. "Daddy," you said, "Eileen cannot go home, she's got to stay here this weekend." That was the beginning of a wonderful relationship with her that is still very strong today, over 20 years later. Debbie, I don't know if you realize it, but you saved her life. Do you think she would be where she is today, mother, wife, special education teacher, best friend, without you?

During the past 16 years since your affliction, first with Lupus, then Scleroderma, how you have been an inspiration for so many people who you have touched. All the folks in the L.A. Lupus Group, first Nancy and then all the others. I remember when we both went to the Lupus Convention in Chicago as delegates, you from L.A. and me from N.J. The great times we had together, but all the time touching other peoples' lives. How you fought for over four years to prove that Lupus patients cannot be stepped on. How your victory was not only a personal victory, but an inspiration for all others to follow your lead, whenever they were being taken advantaged of or discriminated against.

Debbie, I can go on and on with story after story of how much I love you, how proud I have been and am of you, and how important you are to me and all those other people you have touched throughout your life.

Just so you know, I love you, I love you, I love you.

Daddy

Debbie's Gifts (Aunt Rose and Uncle Murray)

We have many wonderful memories of Debbie. What follows is a sampling of a few of the gifts she gave to us which make her so special in our hearts.

The gifts of thoughtfulness and generosity. We remember fondly Debbie playing her guitar at our 25th anniversary party, her making special dishes for us when she stayed with us, buying the foods we liked when we visited her in Israel, as well as giving up her bedroom for us and cooking us a traditional Sabbath dinner.

The gift of emotional warmth. We remember the time when Debbie was a young child and her parents had to leave for a family emergency. Rose came over to help out for a while. We will never forget the wonderful note Debbie wrote saying how much she loved Rose for being there.

The gift of caring. Debbie had a special sensitivity towards those who were hurting. We remember clearly when we were in Israel and Rose injured her ankle at an archeological dig. Debbie was staying with us that night at the hotel and she insisted that we get ice for the ankle and called room service herself to make sure that we got it.

The gifts of patience and forbearance. We remember that despite long years of physical suffering, that Debbie rarely complained. She was an inspiration to how one can deal with long-term chronic illness.

The gift of friendship. Debbie seemed to make friends wherever she went. People always were happy to see her and she brought smile to their faces. When she was showing us around Karmiel, we were often stopped on the streets by people who wanted to talk with her.

The gift of loving. We could go on and on about Debbie's many gifts, but to us this one encompassed all the others. Debbie had a great and marvelous way of making us feel very special and loved. We miss her very much.

The Dream

During the first year after Debbie passed away, I had many vivid dreams about Debbie and they were all very beautiful and wonderful. I still have dreams about her today. This one particular dream that I am going to share with you is the dream that has made the greatest impact of all the dreams I have had. It is also the one dream that I shared at Debbie's unveiling—the dedication of her headstone—in Israel, a year after she passed away.

You know how real dreams are, so you can imagine the feeling that went through me when this dream came about.

The dream opens with Debbie and me sitting in a room with her coming to me saying, "I have an appointment with a doctor today. I will see you in a few hours." This was not unusual, for during all the years Debbie was afflicted with lupus and scleroderma, she had many visits with doctors. The dream continues with Debbie and me embracing and then she leaves to see her doctor. When Debbie comes back from the doctor's office, she is not looking good at all and so I go over to her, grab her, hold her and say, "What is wrong? What did the doctor say?"

Debbie said, "Daddy, the doctor told me that I have lung cancer and I only have a few months to live." I began crying uncontrollably, just continued to cry and cry with her in my arms and tears just rolling down my face and yelling, "Debbie, please, Debbie, Debbie." And then she said, "Daddy, why are you crying, why are you crying," and I said, "Debbie, I can't believe it, I won't believe it," and she said, "Daddy think about this. Don't think about death, think about all the years, think about the fact that we had 36 beautiful, wonderful years together and think about how many children, how many daughters can say that about their relationship with their fathers. How many daughters can say we had 36 beautiful, wonderful years together." The dream ended and I woke up. I woke up in a cold sweat and I quickly woke up Pearl in the middle of the night and said, "I just had this wonderful dream and I have to share it with you." It was this dream that I shared at the unveiling of Debbie's stone in Israel, 1997, one year after she passed away. This is the dream I have shared with many of you, the members of The Compassionate Friends, close friends and relatives. In many ways, this dream has kept me going—"that we had 36 beautiful and wonderful years together." "How many children can say that of their relationship with their fathers."

As I write these words my hand moves to a charm that is hanging on a chain around my neck and the charm has a number on it. The number is 10-1/2. The charm was left to me in Debbie's will and in that will she wrote the following: "I give this 10-1/2 charm to my father, for in all my life he was always more than a 10-1/2 to me". Just for you, Debbie to know in all my life I will never, ever forget my beautiful daughter, and I will never, ever remove that 10-1/2 from around my neck.

Today is the First Day of the Rest of Your Life... Our Special Message (Pearl's Story)

It was approximately 6 months after Debbie left us that something very unusual happened. I call what happened a very spiritually uplifting experience for me, one I will never forget. Still today, after almost seven years, this experience lives inside me and gives me a warm feeling whenever I think about it. I do think about it more often than I would like to admit.

 I had arrived home from work and knew Moe would not be at home since he had a scheduled appointment at the dentist. I went directly to our bedroom and saw a note from Moe sitting on my dresser with the words, *"Today is the first day of the rest of your life."* I thought, how sweet, he left me a special note. Moe has a great habit of listening to our answering machine and jotting down the messages on a nearby pad, but then also saving them on the answering machine for me so that I can hear them, too, when I get home. That day was no exception. I glanced down at the machine and saw the light blinking only once which told me I had only one message to hear. I hit the button and started to move around the room when suddenly I froze in my place. The words that I heard were the words Moe had written on the note he left me: *"Today is the first day of the rest of your life"* but the voice was all too familiar, it was Debbie's voice. I couldn't believe what I was hearing: there was no hello or goodbye, the voice just spoke the words "Today is the first day of the rest of your life." I listened to this message over and over again, thinking, how did Moe ever leave the house and go to the dentist, after he heard this message, Debbie's voice. I continued to play the message over and over and every time I was more convinced it was Debbie, without a doubt. I paced the floor waiting for Moe to arrive home. Finally he walked through the door and I greeted him with, "Did you hear the message and who do you think it sounds like?" His response was very clear and deliberate, "I know it sounds like Debbie's voice, but you know that cannot be, it just has a similar sound." Well, at that point, I knew nothing of the sort. I played it for Moe again and again said, "Listen to the voice—it is Debbie's." Well, he finally said, It sure does sound like her but you know that cannot be so," but this time his words were not so firm. I knew he was having second thoughts that maybe, just maybe, it was Debbie.

I believe with all my heart it was Debbie reaching out to us and wanting us to remember to live the rest of our lives and not waste a day. My thoughts on this matter are that it was a phenomenon that cannot be explained and I am very O.K. with that. I am happy I have this very special and meaningful message to hold in my heart from Debbie. "TODAY IS THE FIRST DAY OF THE REST OF YOUR LIFE."

Thank you, Debbie, for always being able to take me back to what is important in life. You have taught me that it is not how long we live on this earth but how well we live our life while on this earth. You are a great example of a life well lived.

P.S. That evening I called the phone company inquiring if a call could be traced if it was on your answering phone, the answer was no and yes. I did dial *69 to hear the number of the last incoming call but the recording stated it was outside our calling area.

Debbie's Team (Softball and Picnic to Commemorate Debbie's 38th Birthday)

We at The Compassionate Friends talk about many different things during our chapter meetings, among them: how do we cope each day with the loss of a child? Although each day without our loved ones is painful, there are even more special days that come throughout the year. How do we deal with birthdays, how do we cope with his/her absence at Christmas, Hanukkah or Thanksgiving; how do we deal with the anniversary date of his/her passing? All of these are topics that we talk about in our various friendship circles. It was during the first year, Pearl and I were at The Compassionate Friends, that we knew eventually there would be a first anniversary of Debbie's birthday, August 9, 1997. What are we going to do? We always celebrated her birthday. We have talked about how special her birthdays have been throughout this book, and now this would be the first birthday without Debbie. Pearl and I were agonizing over what we wanted to do and how we wanted to do it. Do you celebrate or do you commemorate? We will always remember her, we remember her everyday but as I indicated, there are special days and this is such a special day, the day of her birth, the day I will always remember.

One of the things that we had decided while we were in Israel during the period of shiva, was that we wanted to memorialize her in Israel. Debbie was never married or had children, but she loved children. Pearl and I came up with the idea connected with the synagogue that Debbie was very involved with in Israel and that she helped develop and build. We thought that funding a children's library and activity center at that synagogue in Debbie's name would be most appropriate. We would have books and activities in both Hebrew and English, since the synagogue did attract people from the English speaking part of Karmiel as well as "sabra" or native Israelis. We had by August, 1997, collected a great amount of money to begin the process of funding that children's library. We thought maybe we could do two things to commemorate Debbie's birthday. Debbie loved sports and there are so many stories in this book relating to her love of sports, especially baseball. So what more proper, fitting or appropriate way to commemorate August 9, 1997, which would have been her 38th birthday, than to have a softball game and picnic.

Pearl and I, with the help of Peter, our friend, a graphic artist, who then worked at the New York Power Authority, where I also had worked, designed a tee shirt with "Debbie's Team" Logo, a baseball diamond and the date of her birth – August 9th, 1959 printed on the shirt. We decided to give these shirts to everyone who attended and participated in this picnic. Whoever wanted to contribute, could make a donation to Debbie's Library Fund. This would be a day for friends and family alike, a day to commemorate Debbie's life, on her birthday. August 9th, 1997 turned out to be a very warm and beautiful day and more than 100 people gathered

Moe, Eileen and Jeff

To Honor Debbie Liss
A Celebration of her Birthday!

Marathon Softball Game and Picnic

Saturday, August 9th

Memorial Softball Field
Elmwood Park, NJ
(Market Street & Boulevard)

2:00 PM 'til Dark

Everyone Welcome to Participate!!
(Please bring folding Chairs and Softball Gloves)

We have established a fund in Debbie's memory to benefit Kehilat Hakerem, Karmiel, a Children's Library in Israel

Invitation to Debbie's Baseball Game

at Memorial Field in Elmwood Park, N.J. to play ball, tell stories, picnic and reflect on Debbie's life. I remember I was on the pitcher's mound just about ready to begin the game when I made a short introduction thanking everyone who was there, and said, "we do not need any umpires today because Debbie is here to watch over us" and then I threw out the first pitch. For the next 4 or 5 hours we all enjoyed ourselves, with a tear in our eyes as we commemorated and honored Debbie with a marathon softball game. People just came in and out, oldsters and youngsters, friends, family, work associates, they came from far and near, to be there for our family. It was a wonderful day honoring Debbie.

The Mets Flag

We have talked about Debbie's love for baseball and the New York Mets. In fact, we can say she was fanatical about the Mets. When Debbie moved to Israel she asked that Pearl and I videotape Mets games for her, as well as the Knicks, Rangers and Giants—but most of all the Mets. We would tape a game for her and after taping, if her team won, we would send the game; and if they lost, we would just tape over it and not send it. She only wanted to see the tapes of winning games. In the summer of 1998, with the advent of inter-league play, the Mets were going to play the New York Yankees at Shea Stadium.

I am a member of a men's group called the Spartans, a group that I had first contact with when I was 18 and they were 10 and 11 years old. I was a counselor at Camp Veritans and they were my campers. We organized a boys' club in 1951 still going strong today, as a men's group. Every year for the past 10 or 15 years the Spartan would go to a Mets game. We enjoy the tailgate party before the game as much as the game itself. The first of the inter-league baseball games were played in 1998, and the Mets and Yankees were now playing a home-and-home series. This gave all the members of the Spartans who were Yankees fans an opportunity to see their favorite team, also.

As mentioned, the highlight of the day or the evening, and this was a Sunday night game, was the tailgate party. We had about 50 or 60 people attend that particular game and everyone bought food for the tailgate party. What I normally did for the party was go to an Italian bakery in Garfield, NJ and get semolina bread. We would then make heroes out of this semolina bread. The morning of that particular Sunday in July, 1998, I was on my way to Garfield to pick up the bread; Pearl was on her way to get some other items for the tailgate. It should be noted that the Yankees in the mid to late nineties were *the* team—the class of both leagues; and they had already beaten the Mets twice that weekend, Friday night and Saturday afternoon. I was a little down, but I was very confident that the Mets would win Sunday night. On my way to the bakery in Garfield I passed a garden shop.

On the outside of the garden shop were flags, of various kinds that people hang in front of their homes. It just so happened that they had a Yankee flag and a Mets flag along with many others. I drove by looking at the flags when all of a sudden I stopped short— it was like a message came to me from Debbie saying, "Daddy go back and buy that Mets flag." Sure enough, I backed up, pulled into the shop's driveway to purchase that Mets flag. The owner said, "You know that is the last Mets flag we have. There has been such a run on Mets flag this summer, we do not have any more." I said, "It is very important that I buy a Mets flag, can you give me the one hanging outside?" She said, "I do not really like to, because it is a display flag, but we should be getting more soon so I will sell it to you."

As soon as I arrived home, I replaced the flag we had outside our home with this new Mets flag. When Pearl came home she said, "I don't remember having a Mets flag there. What happened?" I told her the story about Debbie's voice inside me telling me to buy that Mets flag and then I said, "You know something, I believe that the Mets are going to win tonight and I believe they are going to win for Debbie and not only do I believe they are going to win, I know they are going to win. I really am so, so confident that they are going to win tonight that I am going to tell everyone. I will tell everyone at the tailgate the story of the flag, Debbie's voice and the fact that the Mets are guaranteed to win."

We now head to Shea Stadium and the parking lot for our tailgate party. We are all gathering, some of the Yankee fans bring little brooms—the brooms represent "sweep." Whenever a team wins the first two games of a three-game series the fanatics of that team bring brooms to the game to indicate that they are going to sweep. The Yankee fans were really getting on me saying that hey, we are going to sweep you tonight, the Yankees are going to take three. My response was very simple, "You know there is no way you guys can win tonight," and I proceeded to tell the story of Debbie, her voice, and the Mets flag. They all knew Debbie, they respected my feelings and the pain I was going through. However, tonight there was no pain, just a strong feeling that Debbie was here with us and that her magic would overcome any adversity tonight and the Mets would win.

After our tailgate party, we all went into the game and it really was a great game—a tight pitcher's battle that lasted until the bottom of the 9th inning. The score was tied one to one and I believe everyone of the 55,000 fans there were still in the park, it was such an exciting game. I was very confident and I knew that the Mets were going to win in the last of the 9th inning. Wouldn't you know it, the Mets scored a run in their final turn at bat, and won the game two to one and I remember saying to everyone at the game, "Debbie was here. They won for Debbie, the Mets won for Debbie."

Letters to Dad from Jeff

Dear Dad

Hi! I wrote this after I watched Simon Birch one night. I learned that the two times a person has the most energy is when they come in and when they leave. If you would like to share this, it is your choice. I am hoping that it will be read at the gravesite.

May the light support you in these next few weeks and always.

Love,
Jeff

Friday, August 6, 1999

"For when someone leaves the pain continues. All the years coming up in the strangest of times. A movie, a song, baseball game, dinner, holidays in laughter and sadness, it's always there.
For a hole is never filled by the leaving of another. The rain comes down the cheeks through the families' eyes. The silence and hush moments of that missing piece the hole that can't be filled the hole that can't be filled.
The smile that was there through the years and that special laugh the hole that can't be filled.
Old pictures, movies, songs that seem so real but are only illusions to the hole that can't be filled.
Love is so important, for no one knows when you will have the hole that can't be filled.

Letter to Moe from Shannon, a close friend of Debbie's

January 25, 1999

Dear Moe

What a delight to receive your letter! You have no idea how it cheered me to hear from you.

How I got to Boston is a long story, but Debbie had quite a bit to do with it, so I'll share the highlights. PennCorp was purchased by a trio who then took it public, purchased Occidental of North Carolina, then moved the operations and the Santa Monica management to North Carolina to train the existing staff. Then they laid all of us off after three months. It was devastating to say the least. (It made me reassess how I handled Debbie's departure from the company and I was ashamed that I had not been more supportive. I suppose I was trying to protect my position and reputation with the company, a cowardly motive to say the least and one that I will never repeat.) In retrospect, it was the best thing that could have happened to me. Had I not been laid off, I probably would have stayed there until I retired, doing a job I didn't like, working for people I didn't trust, living in a state for which I didn't care.

I was in Milton-Freewater, Oregon, living with my mother, working as a "girl Friday" at a local real estate office. I liked the people and the work was challenging, but not my niche. This is where I was when Debbie's brother Jeff called me and told me Debbie had passed away.

The news sent me reeling. I was surprised, hurt, angry, and mystified. To be quite honest, in a lot of ways I still am. After the initial shock, oodles of prayers and some reluctant closures, I remembered something very critical that Jeff had said during our discussion. "Debbie was doing everything she wanted to, she had finally found things that made her happy." What a wake up call! This made me reconsider my life and recognize that I was not doing what I wanted to, nor was I happy. While I can't say I was visited by her spirit, or saw any great light shows, or heard her voice in the night, I know that if Debbie could have said anything to me it would have been, "Do something you love. Don't settle. Take whatever risks you need to, but do it. Life is short."

For years I had planned to attend culinary school, "some time in the future." I finally understood that the future becomes the present. It comes and goes without my permission or acknowledgement. I contacted several schools then enrolled full time at the Western Culinary Institute in Portland, Oregon. I graduated in April with the highest cumulative GPA in the history of the school. I met hundreds of wonderful people. I learned a great deal. I am profiled in this year's annual report as one of the most successful graduates. It was a dream come true.

Following graduation, I was the executive chef at Wapiti Meadow Ranch, an upscale guest ranch in Idaho's Wilderness of No Return. Great job! Wonderful people. Beautiful country. Finally, I was making a living doing what I loved. What a relief. What a joy. How easy and simple once I just moved forward.

At the end of the season, I moved to Boston to become a consultant with the Jacob Wirth Company Restaurant, and that's how I ended up in Boston and no, I am not a Red Sox Fan, my heart will always be with the San Francisco Giants.

I don't regret the "career change" for one moment. While all the hard work is mine, Debbie's physical death prompted my change. My professional happiness, success and achievements are her legacy to me.

Love
Shannon

Afterthoughts

For those of you, out there, who would like to become more sensitive to those of us who have lost a child, here are some simple "do's" and "don'ts":

Do's

Do ask us about our loss and ask to hear stories about our child (children). Many of us love to tell stories about our loved ones.

Do understand that *we are different from you* and will never be "whole" again or the "same" as we once were.

Do come close to us and extend your hand to us. We need both your understanding and compassion.

Do keep the friendships and relationships. We don't want to be isolated and alone.

Don'ts

Don't tell us, "We know how you feel." We don't want you to ever know how we feel. Only those who have lost a child can, know how we feel."

Don't tell us, "Time will heal", or "Time ALWAYS heals." Nothing heals the loss of a child. Not time, people, places or things.

Don't tell us, "I feel your pain." Our pain is so individual, that many times, even our dearest loved ones, can't feel my pain, nor I hers.

Don't withdraw when you see us cry, become silent or act in some other way that may not seem appropriate at that time. The incident at hand may have brought back a fond or sad memory of our loved ones. Our actions become spontaneous, regardless of their appropriateness.

Afterwards

After the Death of a Child

How does a parent continue to go on with life after he or she loses a child? How does he/she live when a piece of him or her is no longer with them. They talk about healing: you have a wound and it is healed; you have a hurt and it is healed. There is pain and then there is healing. Well, there is no healing when you lose a child; you just don't heal. The pain, in many cases, gets even greater. The hole that is inside you is never filled. How does one go on? How does one find meaning in life when one loses a child? What you learn from those of us who are members of The Compassionate Friends or other support groups, is that life in itself has meaning. To go on living is what is meaningful. You go on living because you know that your loved one would want you to continue. I mean, Debbie would really be "pissed" if she knew that I had done something tragically to myself as a result of her passing. This father does not want to have a daughter who is "pissed." You learn that life goes on, a different kind of life. You learn that you go on because your loved one would want you to go on. You also learn you go on because of the loved ones that are still here, in my case, beautiful wife Pearl, my other children, Brenda, Jaime, Jeff, who need a father, grandchildren who want a grandfather, relatives and friends who want to remain close to you and you, yourself, because you do really want to go on living even with this great pain, even with this hole inside you. Knowing that this hole, filled with the pain, will never go away. What you really learn, as you continue on with your life after the death of a child—you learn how to cope, you learn different coping strategies that help you live from one day to another. For me, one of my coping strategies centered around Debbie's Stories. They have kept me alive these years after her passing and they will continue to keep me alive as I continue telling Debbie's Stories.

I wrote this book, first as a tribute to my daughter, and second to dedicate it to all of you out there who have lost a child and know the real meaning of life. I wrote this book as part therapy, part coping. I wrote this book so that I could continually read *Debbie's Stories*, get a laugh, shed a tear, feel warm inside and feel the pain. I wrote *Debbie's Stories* so that those of you who are reading it now, maybe can feel something that may help you continue on, if you have lost a child, or if you haven't, you will have a better understanding of what life is like for us. Maybe you won't say to someone, a friend, a family member, associate, colleague, "Tell me, are you getting any better?" "Tell me, is there any less pain?" "Tell me, how is your healing coming?" Maybe you will realize that there is no healing, that the pain doesn't get any easier. Maybe it will help you understand us better, that we are just different.

For those of you who are reading this book who have lost a child, those of you who are members of The Compassionate Friends or other organizations, I reach out to you and say you understand my pain as I understand your pain and hopefully you have gained something from reading this book. Not only a picture about Debbie and her father, and relatives and friends, but, hopefully, it helped you cope better. If it helped you deal with your life and the meaning of your life if it gave you a smile or even a laugh, if it helped you cope with your loss even in the smallest way, then the book has served its purpose.

In conclusion and summary, I want to take this opportunity to thank everyone who helped and contributed to *Debbie's Stories*. First and foremost, to my wonderful wife Pearl who stood by me all these years and who has shared my pain. I want to thank her not only for being there but for all the work that she did to make *Debbie's Stories* possible. For transcribing, helping with editing, for adding her stories to the book—for all of this and much, much more. To all the other members of my family for being there for me and adding to this book, I want to thank you. For all of Debbie's friends who have contributed to this book, thank you for your support and making this book possible.

A special thank you to Jane Janovsky for her artistic creativity in designing the cover.

Finally, for those of you out there who have taken the time to read the stories, thank you—thank you for being there, thank you for sharing *Debbie's Stories* with me and thank you for allowing me to share a part of my life with you.

www.ingramcontent.com/pod-product-compliance
Lightning Source LLC
Chambersburg PA
CBHW021014090426
42738CB00007B/784